B Sharp!

Your personal music journey

to expand the mind,

enhance the brain,

and age well

Philip Maffetone

B Sharp!

*Your personal music journey
to expand the mind,
enhance the brain, and age well*

David Barmore Productions

Copyright 2023 by Philip Maffetone

ISBN 9798398386073

Edited by Hal Walter
Line editing by Sharon Skye Forest
Cover art by Maryna Yakovchuk

Philip Maffetone's music website:
www.MaffetoneMusic.com

Table of Contents

Introduction 5
1. It Was 20 Years Ago Today 9
2. Awakening Dreams 13
3. The Amazing Journey 19
4. The Art of Science is Music 27
5. The Indispensable 37
6. Embrace the Lazy Brain 47
7. Learning, Playing and Plasticity 57
8. The Five-Minute Power Break 69
9. Music Soothes the Aging Brain 77
10. Rewire and Reorganize 85
11. It's a Jungle Out There 97
12. Our Musical Personalities 109
13. Once Upon a Time: Beyond Storytelling 119
14. Sharing Song Stories 131
15. Singer-Songwriter Narratives 139
16. The Music of Exercise and Sport 157
17. The Meditative Dance 171
18. Sex, Drugs, Rock 'n' Roll . . . and Food 179
19. Heart Health and Music 199
20. If Tomorrow Never Comes 205

Introduction
Why this Book is Unique

If happy little bluebirds fly beyond the rainbow, why, oh why, do we need music to take us there? The mind loves it. And science now knows how music can heal us. Do we dare to dream about these boundless benefits for a better brain-body? Can simple methods encourage it? Yes, that's what this book is about.

Music listening quickly expands the mind. The benefits increase when music is further personalized with toe tapping, singing along, seeing it performed, and even more by dancing, writing or playing it. The process goes beyond pulling our heartstrings, feeling forever young, and getting more love from life. Music can improve personality, protect and repair the brain, and widen our horizons to inspire more personal human potential. That's just the beginning.

It began with our earliest ancestors. We're all born to listen, sing, create and move to music. As babies, it facilitates communication and bonding with our mothers, synchronizing the brain to regulate intellect, behavior and body movements of those around us. Music contributes to maturation through awareness of empathy, compassion, cooperation and trust, facilitating a powerful social influence connecting all humans as a single family.

Humanity's story *is* music.

It's probably in your head right now, with us consciously and subconsciously even when we sleep. The melodies, harmonies, rhythms and the magic of music's veracity can potentially teach us to listen, share and live in the moment.

This book is my story, woven within yours as a stream of newborn music heard over and over again. Essential to survival — like sex and food — it's inseparable, nourishing and a natural driving human force. Shakespeare wrote, "If music be the food of love, play on."

But has music gone astray? If so, it could impair us personally, as a population and a planet. Changes in human music appear to parallel increasing global rates of brain injuries that can cloud communication and cognition. When this occurs in songbirds, scientists show, it signals extinction.

Just like art and science, and brain and body, the mind and music are one. From the beginning it guided us to superspecies stardom. Now, the expressive power of song can help rescue us and our planet.

In his recent book, *The Creative Act: A Way of Being*, music producer Rick Rubin states, "Your entire life is a form of self-expression. You exist as a creative being in a creative universe. A singular work of art."

Can we build a better brain, *really*? Create a *new you*? Most definitely, for everyone of all ages — musician or not. Various time-tested clinical methods featured herein help us rapidly and continuously expand the mind by renewing the brain through a natural process called *neuroplasticity*. All our physical and mental experiences enable plasticity, especially learning and enlisting memories. Music may be the most powerful way to accomplish this throughout our lifespan, not just to keep our mind sharp but to develop and further expand it.

Music can quickly boost alpha and theta brainwaves, inducing a state much like deep meditation. It also can promote optimal aging, protect and repair the brain, produce new brain cells and maximize brain-body health. Moreover, music can powerfully manage the effects of our daily physical, biochemical and mental-emotional stress through the brain's natural neurohormonal HPA axis.

Many know me as a clinician who, for decades in health, sports, nutrition and biofeedback developed many self-care methods, published research and wrote books. Singer-songwriter James Taylor said, "Dr. Maffetone's system goes beyond dealing with symptoms; he looks at health and fitness as an integrated balance. He deals with the whole picture clearly and directly."

At the peak of this wonderful clinical career, I woke one day with the overwhelming yearning to write songs. The passion to exclusively pursue this personal creative artistic endeavor as a songwriter became a journey beyond musical mind expansion. It saved my life.

Music can enhance or save your life too. Thanks to a rich musical past, passed down by the earliest humans, we all have the power to expand the mind, write the score and uncover more of ourselves, and improve health with music.

Whether you're a novice musician, retain bad memories of music lessons, dream to play and improve, or are wildly successful and still want more, everyone can go where no human brain has gone before.

There is no better time to expand the mind than now. Being healthier humans on a peace-loving planet is a reality when we dare to dream the dreams that come true.

— Philip Maffetone

1
It Was 20 Years Ago Today

We all have a story to tell. I want to share one of mine to explain how I got here. It began 20 years ago at the time of this writing.

One day I woke as a songwriter. This moment was not in my youth but in midlife, at the peak of a totally different career. Waking as a songwriter was an organic act, it just happened, unplanned. The passion was so intense I would abandon my decades-long profession and become engulfed in music.

It still feels like yesterday. I was at the height of a celebrated career that included traveling the world to work in the field of human health and performance, coaching athletes, and lecturing, researching and writing extensively on the subject. The passion for music was suddenly so intense that everything else came crashing down that morning of April 14, 2002.

I was struck with a feeling of embarrassment and sadness that I had ignored something so essential for my entire life. Promoting healthy living through nutrition, physical activity and creative thinking was all great, but something was clearly lacking in my essential being. This awakening would uncover another important aspect of my life.

Our earliest ancestors made music, and for tens of thousands of generations along the way this was a special and necessary human practice. However, until this moment, *creating* it eluded me. Being a heavy consumer of great music suddenly felt selfish. It was as though I'd been taking without giving back. All this quickly faded away as I began to write.

Looking back, it's evident I spent my early years of life with an undiagnosed but significant brain injury. Today, this might be given a label like autism spectrum disorder. I found schoolwork difficult, failing each year and having to take classes every summer. But what was interesting is that my poor brain function also included what later was understood as a condition called *amusia* — difficulty and confusion relating to music. Songs would sometimes be played in our home, on a radio or vinyl records. These included classical pieces, and some that my mother practiced on piano to learn her choir parts, which always sounded painful to me. It was not until years later that I realized she was practicing harmonies not melodies. Hearing classmates perform music made me feel left out. I wasn't just uncomfortable, but also frustrated I could not even sing or dance, tap a beat with a finger or foot, or produce the right notes on rudimentary instruments, such as a plastic flute that the whole class had to play at one time. Despite talking very little and never asking questions, at some point in middle school some urge led me to ask about learning music. I was told my grades were not good enough to add more studies.

The Beatles' appearance on the Ed Sullivan show grabbed my attention, but I didn't know what to make of that experience other than being unable to stop thinking about it. Suddenly the popular songs I heard my older brother listening to on the car radio made sense. That was the beginning of my music listening world.

Sometime later, a friend showed me how to play three chords on his electric guitar, even though he didn't have an amplifier. It got me thinking about playing, and after making some money from mowing lawns I bought a $15 guitar, which only ended in frustration despite having a songbook or two. I remember joking that maybe I should write my own songs so no one would know if I was playing them correctly or not. Through later adolescence and into adulthood my experiences and experimentations helped my brain evolve and expand with wide ranges of daily music listening taking the lead.

Flash forward several decades and writing music unleashed a refreshing and intense experience, an energy never felt before. It was a feeling of creation that required expression — one I had to transform into a song.

The thought of being without music was suddenly frightening. Imagine preventing a songbird or a whale from singing. Over time, my songwriting evolution expanded and improved, with feedback from my longtime music mentor, producer Rick Rubin, and discussions with Johnny Cash, and others in music. Ironically, I had made these contacts because of work in my previous career, providing the feeling of a natural progression that led to finding myself. It was just another steppingstone.

As the years passed, recording, and performing live added more flame to my creative fires. Little did I know at the time that expanding my creativity to learn music and become a singer-songwriter as my primary focus would eventually come full circle. Not only did it help me in many mental-emotional and physical ways, it expanded my sense of purpose, and literally saved my life. Putting all the pieces together would allow me to share these experiences to help many other people expand their minds to have healthier brains and bodies. Another stop along this journey is the creation of this book.

Navigating these extremes from amusia to writing songs helped me better understand balance, a process I continue to strive for today. Perhaps becoming a songwriter was the most important step into my brave new world. I was no longer isolated or alone. I felt the joy of shared humanity. Music had always been a part of who I was, but now it was who I was becoming. It all seemed so new with each song, then and now, as if the future kept being foretold.

2

Awakening Dreams

Most of us have several dreams each night, which occur during REM (rapid eye movement) sleep, although we often don't recall them. Creative brains appear to dream more. Did I dream about becoming a songwriter? My sleep-wake transition usually includes relaxing in the theta brain wave meditative state for a little while before opening my eyes and thinking about the day. This healthier transition can also help one to remember dreams, although there was no recall of one on that morning.

Our wandering daydreams share similar brain relationships with those at night, reflecting a creative brain that loves to dream especially while on autopilot.

The notion that we are all unique individuals has always been a cornerstone of my life's work long before music became the focus. After realizing there were no instructions for creativity, including writing new songs, the real lesson was that the music was always within, already a part of my own being. The feelings, energies, tears, and all else can thrust you onto a stage with a song you perform by being just yourself. Not that being oneself was always easy before. Celebrating my individuality would only be amplified with songwriting.

Beyond Dreams

Music is more individual than a fingerprint, more potent than a psychedelic. It can leap above our busy world and reveal a hidden rainbow of dreams beyond. The birth of every new, never-before-heard song is an original mind-altering moment that furthers its predecessor, never tiring, adding even more fuel to the passion. How amazing that a small handful of musical notes can create virtually unlimited melodies, an endless array of newfound songs streaming across our universe.

Songwriting also opened a new listening experience. The power of music goes both ways. Suddenly I was enjoying music in an expanded form. Just listening nurtures the subconscious mind. Songs, like other waking conscious activities, can even appear in our dreams.

These days, almost daily, I take some time to lie down and purely listen to music while entering a dreamy state. It's often a whole album from a singer-songwriter or band, or a new artist I've never heard before. It's a moving, emotional experience, as these sessions also typically bring me into a deep alpha and theta meditation. Occasionally listening to some of my own recordings can also bring tears of joy.

In fact, just like many other creations, songs can often be inspired by dreams. Whether waking in the middle of one or during that twilight state while drifting into sleep or upon awakening, many songs come to us as a feeling or sensation from the subconscious mind. It's not unlike that vague memory we have when waking from a vivid dream, which some even believe are insights to other dimensions. Sometimes, even though you cannot quite recall the dream, you may find the memory of it has affected your mood. You may even partially piece the dream back together later in the day. Other times you might wonder if you have rewritten the dream, or added to it in your waking mind, to suit your own reality. Humans most likely have been translating these sensations from their earliest evolutions, expressing and sharing them as songs.

Is this how we can more easily touch our subconscious mind, and interpret, decipher, and share it with others? If this healthy creative expression results in a work of art, it is a viable and valuable form of communication and understanding.

By expressing a subconscious feeling to create a song, we become aware and conscious of it. While it appears that hearing the songs of others, especially when we can see ourselves in the song as we often do, we also become conscious of that (original) subconscious feeling, at least in some form.

These are among the many important benefits discussed in this book — to expand the mind, reach into the subconscious state, and improve brain performance while spreading the joys of music. We can share both the conscious and subconscious aspects of our mental state, and still maintain individuality. A shared consciousness may best be accomplished through creative expressions that also reveal the subconsciousness too. Not only can this help us personally, but it could also improve the health of society, and the planet as well.

Along the way I learned that the song is not the passion, or a potion; the power is the passion hidden in the song, awaiting a shared exposure of our subconscious feeling brought to consciousness through creative expression. It's a celebration of creation, one to experience daily.

So, let's fill our spaces with them every day. Why wait to celebrate anything? Music *is* the party!

Daydreams

While it may seem like fiction, mental time travel into our past and future is as real as the dreams we dare to dream by day, and perfectly normal.

> *Case History: He was fond of daydreaming in school, forgetful, had problems with social interaction, and exhibited repetitive patterns of behavior. A loner, he repeated sentences, hated the strict protocols and rote learning demanded by teachers, but would become a good musician. Today he might be diagnosed with ADHD or autism, later saying that "Imagination is more important than knowledge," emphasizing, "knowledge is limited*

whereas imagination embraces the entire world, stimulating progress, giving birth to evolution."

In what may have started as a daydream, he theorized the existence of undetectable gravitational waves emanating from black holes in space. His brain translated mental representations into mathematical equations, developing a scientific explanation for them.

Scientists recently announced the first detection of these gravitational waves from two merging black holes in faraway space, confirming Albert Einstein's century-old General Theory of Relativity.

Daydreaming: Einstein did it, Michelangelo too, and most others who have contributed creatively original ideas and discoveries. Psychoanalyst Sigmund Freud first introduced his theory of the unconscious with respect to nighttime dream interpretation in his 1899 book, *The Interpretation of Dreams*. Philosopher Richard Rorty wrote that self-knowledge is a matter of getting acquainted with and listening to this inner self — it's the "crazy quasi people" who share what's inside our brains. We consciously learn something from them, converse with other versions of us, even agree to disagree, expand our minds, and alter our behaviors from it, all for the better. Such is the feature of a healthy brain.

We daydream from the earliest age, probably even before birth. Children can get lost in their minds for hours virtually anywhere. We all daydream stories, games, and journeys that can lead to philosophy, inventions, music, paintings and billion-dollar businesses. However, this is frowned upon rather than encouraged in school. It's no surprise that young students who struggle in school can become successful because they're highly creative adults schooled through daydreams.

Scientists say adults spend up to 50 percent of our day dreaming, often entertaining social stories that may help regulate emotions, increase positive feelings towards ourselves, and fantasize.

Maladaptive daydreaming is a *daymare*, a terrifying experience found in a very small number of unhealthy patients. It's associated with depression, dysphoria, anxiety, or other symptoms of mental illness.

We're meant to dream, so keep on dreaming on. And we belong in each other's dreams. As Bob Dylan said: "I'll let you be in my dreams if I can be in yours."

3

The Amazing Journey

I began performing my songs publicly, sometimes while lecturing on the topic of music and the brain. I would tell my story about waking as a songwriter and leaving behind my previous career to follow this passion. Sometimes the responses were sad or envious: "*I wish I could do that!*" was a very common response. No, I was not wealthy, not retiring, nor was it a new hobby to tinker with. While I appreciated the congratulatory comments, what many people were expressing is they could not, or would not, follow their passions, or could only view doing so within a financial construct. Yet I've been fortunate and honored to hear stories about people who did realize their passions and went for it.

A key bridge from my former career to this new one came in the form of an email from music producer Rick Rubin. It arrived just four days after I woke as a songwriter. He just finished reading one of my books and was seeking personal health advice. Talking on the phone, I told him about having just become a songwriter and my new intention to no longer work in the health field. We laughed and after a long conversation agreed to help one another.

Through the conscious mind, our subconscious sometimes finds creative pathways to connect with the right people at the right time. Almost serendipitously I had the good fortune to have some other fine musicians help me along on my journey as well. Soon, I would move to West Hollywood, California, to work with Rick, a relationship that led to many other interesting music connections. It was like a post-doctoral program of wonderfully intense study, eight days a week. While I hoped that these very successful songwriters would show me how to write great songs, they didn't. Instead, something better unfolded. Rather than pushing some persona or musical style upon me, other professional musicians encouraged my individuality to flow out.

Those few years in the Hollywood Hills uniquely impacted my music career. It's where the Laurel Canyon counterculture music revolution was born decades earlier. Many great singer-songwriters still lived nearby, and I began meeting or working with them, and eventually recording my own music in some of the same studios. The experience solidified the love for music I'd first found growing up with the songs of the 1960s.

Often accompanying Rick on his rounds to different sessions and events, we visited studios to hear Neil Diamond, the Red Hot Chili Peppers, Weezer, and others. Working with Stephen Stills, Damien Rice, Dan Wilson and Vincent Gallo, and conversing with Bono and Diane Warren were incredibly great lessons for me. Bob Hilburn, longtime *L.A. Times* rock critic and book author who interviewed me after I worked with Johnny Cash, was also a wonderful influence. Most exciting was when John Frusciante and Brad Wilk showed up in the studio to help me record some of my own songs. Jonny Polonsky was there too, a great creative singer-songwriter with the ability to read my musical mind using his instrumental and vocal prowess.

Of course, Rick Rubin was there in his own special and quiet way, encouraging me to be more of myself, the creative artist. That meant finding where my songs came from.

Where Do Songs Originate?

Many have pondered where the really great songs originate. Some say they come from the soul, referencing Bob Dylan. While Dylan never actually made that claim, he did reference it in the now classic song, "Tangled Up in Blue." One of the song's characters refers to a book of poems from the 13th century. Dylan wrote:

And every one of them words rang true

And glowed like burnin' coal

Pourin' off of every page

Like it was written in my soul from me to you

Not surprisingly, from an early age Dylan read a lot of poetry and other works of fiction. Born Robert Zimmerman, he took his pen name from the poet Dylan Thomas. The Bob Dylan line referenced above apparently refers to the Italian poet Dante and his famous "Divine Comedy." Decades later, in 2016, Dylan would be awarded a Nobel Prize in Literature.

Even before language, human storytelling songs had significant meaning. They were communicated through music's powerful poetic influence on body language, vocal variations, gait and facial expressions. Today, music is still hardwired in our brains from before birth, enabling us to use music as we see fit — listening, playing, writing, dancing or doing it all.

We might say, therefore, that our songs descend from our earliest ancestors, a notion that's in line with the concept of creative subconsciousness put forth by psychologist Carl Jung. We can encourage and allow this creativity to be expressed through our conscious mind; it helps define our individuality, modify it, and even change the world with it.

The excitement of creative expression, even the birth of a single song, can be enough to befuddle the brain in celebratory ways. A story of the great Greek mathematician Archimedes is telling. He was challenged by the problem of determining the volume of an irregularly shaped item. Getting into a bathtub one day as the water level rose, he suddenly realized that the volume and density of an object could be measured based on the amount of water it displaced. Legend has him shouting "Eureka!" with such excitement he ran out of the house naked because he forgot to dress.

Using neuroimaging technologies, researchers can now better understand the exciting creative process as it moves from subconscious to conscious to its final expression.

Unfortunately, the background noise of today's society continues impeding the flow of our natural artistic talents, and even the ability for many to enjoy and benefit from music. As Oliver Wendell Holmes, Sr., a poet, physician, professor and scholar, said, *"Alas for those that never sing but die with all their music in them."* It was not our music or storytelling communication that distinguished us from other animals, as these traits were shared with other living creatures. It was our growing creative brains that allowed us to use imagination to express our dreams, our subconsciousness, to help make our existence healthier.

Ultimately, lyrics were added as language evolved making us more unique. Yet it's the music that helps take us beyond the lyrics; even the same words can, and are, interpreted differently by different listeners, helping bring out the individuality of both the creator and receiver as when hearing a song, we often put ourselves in the story.

Language also led to something distinctive in the human brain: fiction. It was the capacity to stretch artistic license, to fib, keep secrets, or use expanding imagination to make up any twist to a story we wish. We became a species of dreamers expressed in all the expanding arts. This continuum of human creativity paralleled brain development, one that began in our early ancestors and continues today.

Similar parallels are observed throughout our own lifetime. As children we are artists from the earliest age, gradually maturing with the brain's creative endeavors and incorporating all that is within us to personalize artistic expression. A healthy, active, creative brain turns out innovative, offbeat storylines and tales with healing powers that we can almost see, feel and touch.

So, the brain is the source of our songs. Yet, even if they come from the supernatural, the feeling of a song must still be translated to creative musical components in the mind, with influence by conscious and subconscious memories that attach meaning and prose. Jung might simply say that artistic expressions articulate our multiple personalities. While our brains are us, our songs express it.

This certainly does not discount spirituality or its institutionalized form, religion. It may not seem to fit the scientific model, but it does. Whether music is written in our soul, from a God above (or below), or in other ways, we express it cognitively. If God sends us a song, he or she does it through the brain.

We are all naturally creative while being uniquely individual. This occurs across all the arts and with shared effects, and feelings of emotional intensities. From poems and song lyrics to symphonies, paintings and sculptures, the brain waves shift into an alpha state upon exposure to art. This brings a feeling of awe that can be measured in a laboratory. Rhyming, melodic repetition, wordless notes of symphonic story, harmonic flow of paint on canvas, a chunk of marble coming to life, are all packaged up as physical and chemical bits in our brain.

For these reasons, we must as a society avoid differentiating between different art forms, such as poetry and lyrics, or categorizing paintings or musical styles. These and other sensibilities — too often inspired by academics or marketing influences — can distract from the pure love of art.

An important part of this amazing journey is understanding how art comes from the freedom of our own special feelings, an essence of individuality. Such features of the human brain, the good, the bad, the in-between, each creative face we feel, are shared and represented as art.

Passion also is a vital feeling connected with art. It drives creativity. Passion urges our brains to be better humans, to "keep on keepin' on" through uniquely consuming and creating art. In modern society, however, too few people now participate in this basic human activity. Artistic passion is not encouraged and often repressed, de-emphasized in education, and no longer a respected endeavor. This book is intended to help readers initiate, restore and expand the passion for creativity. To live without the full spectrum of art in our lives is to not be whole, as Holmes may have inferred. Too many people never experience or allow the passion, the special creative features and feel for the art already within us. Doing so at any age could spark the freedom to feed our human creativity and make the world a better place.

My life's artistic journey began as a teenager, with a major influence of storytelling music from songwriters traveling their own road, spreading musical lyrics in meaningful, heartfelt beautiful songs. In addition to Dylan and the Beatles, I was shaped by the works of Joni Mitchell, the Moody Blues, Cat Stevens, Nina Simone, Leonard Cohen and many others. So, it was only logical that when I woke as a songwriter in mid-life, my personal storytelling style was part of the journey too. My songs reflect rebirth, real love, expanded consciousness, and the interfering intrusion and illusion of society. Of course, lyrics and music are often interpreted differently by listeners, who often parse the moods and memories to fit their own experience or those of others, real or imagined, in the song.

While the songs I write are those that come out of my mind, this passion rallies around a common theme — the crazy notion of love and peace. Thus, my songs may feel happy and sad, playful and teary, heavy or light as a feather.

4

The Art of Science is Music

Artistic creativity is one of the most mysterious forms of human behavior. It's been described in many ways throughout recorded history, even transcending to the metaphysical. Music has the power to immediately change our state of consciousness and enlist the subconscious. These meditative, feel-good, creative healthy states can even be measured as waves of electrical energy in the brain.

To describe this merger of art and science in music is certainly a challenge. It's the intimate, intricate and instinctual unification, the creation of nature. The term music, from the Greek mousiké [tekhnē] refers to the *technique (or art) of the Muses* and follows logical and natural mathematical patterns that can create trillions of unique musical compositions from a mere handful of single notes. These combined variations of melody, harmony, rhythm, pitch, meter, timbre (sound color) and other features can bring us great joy and improved health.

Scientists know this as well. Music has been called a *mnemonic* ruse that quickly, directly or indirectly, cues or activates virtually all areas of the brain to expand the mind. Functional magnetic resonance imaging (fMRI) studies show the brains of musical people are larger and more functional than those of others. Shifting states of consciousness reflected in changing brain waves can be measured by an electroencephalogram (EEG). Music's physical and mental outcomes also are known to influence stress hormones, neurotransmitters, muscle movements and many functions that could promote wellbeing and be harnessed therapeutically.

Thousands of years ago, Chinese Medicine described music as a primary part of society and life, denoting its therapeutic qualities with the traditional Five Elements of musical tones corresponding to *do, re, mi, so, la* in the modern musical scale. The ancient Egyptians also emphasized music in a healthy life, and early Greek philosophers Pythagoras, Aristotle and Plato encouraged the healing and transformative power of music, while discovering the simple mathematics associated with it. Later, biologist Charles Darwin studied and researched human music as a key to sexual selection — finding the best mates — with scientists elaborating more on his work in recent years. In short, when singing, a potential mate sees and hears a reflection of one's brain and body.

In the beginning, human music, not unlike that of most animals, was simple singing and gesturing. Unique to humans was rhythm associated with specialized brain areas that regulate physical movement, and a rhythmic beat associated with walking and running. Hearing and feeling the heartbeat would have led to drum-like actions and dancing. These rhythmic actions are important components of communication and socialization. More components of music paralleled an expanding creative and more effective brain.

Beyond its strong link to cognition, emotions and memory, music is always influencing us. Even during silence, our auditory cortex, where music is first sensed, is active. Whether only sensing music internally or listening, it can still trigger the nerves that move muscles, even if the body appears to be resting.

Tonal Language and Modal Music

Darwin and many modern scholars agree that music preceded language by millions of years and helped in its development.

The earliest human verbal languages were musical, too, appearing between 50,000 and 150,000 years ago. These *tonal* tongues had musical sounds with as much meaning as the words. About 40,000 years ago, tonality began diminishing and today makes up about 40 percent of the world's languages. This includes about 1.5 billion people using them primarily in China, Southeast Asia, sub-Saharan Africa, some indigenous communities in Mexico, the Navajo Nation in the Southwest U.S. and elsewhere.

Tonal language is more musical and mathematical compared to newer tongues using letters and words. Tonal speakers tend to have improved verbal memory and recall, and pitch discrimination. This could be why learning to understand and play music is faster and easier using mathematics rather than the traditional letters (A through G) and words (such as sharp, flat, diminished, etc.) which requires more memorization and less learning. Tonality also encourages *improvisation*, playing naturally with emotion and without musical notation, which can be more joyful and therapeutic.

It's interesting that a baby's brain responds to music even before birth, while learning to understand and use modern language takes much longer. Similarly, songwriters tend to easily recall their melodies, chords and other musical features of new songs, but could take longer, even months or more, to remember the words.

In a similar way that tonal language is older, more natural, and most musical, *modal* music follows similar patterns in human development.

Modes, or modulations, are musical scales with sounds that give more variations of color, character and feel to a musical piece. They can instill a natural element of surprise and build tension to a brilliant resolution. Even when simple, the songs feel more complex and original, with a greater emotional range of deep intellectual content (even before considering the lyrics). Modal sounds seem interesting and different to the brain, even for people who don't know music theory. Hearing is believing — listen to the Beatles "And I Love Her" or my song, "Rosemary."

Modality is exemplified in the oldest music of traditional folk, the songs of Ancient Greece, Gregorian chants, Jewish cantillation, and in some non-Western music, such as

Tibetan chanting. They are prevalent in the compositions of Beethoven, Mozart and other classical greats. For unknown reasons, modes were out of vogue for a period. They surged again during the 1950s with jazz improvisation and expanded during the 1960s folk and rock but began diminishing again afterwards.

The natural feel of modality can help us sense that each genre is very closely related, empowering people to love and reap the benefits of all music.

Does Music *Always* Help Us?

While music has the *potential* to improve the brain-body in spectacular ways, it's not always that simple. When we are affected by some significant stress or an accumulation of stressors, just listening to music may not offset, reduce or eliminate the stress or its effects, although it can help. It's individual. In short, physical, biochemical, and mental-emotional stress can significantly impair health and counter health-promoting factors that might normally help us, including music. But there are things we can do to better benefit from music — including obtaining the required dietary brain nutrients, expanding our musicality and other methods discussed in this book.

Music and Stress

While we are regularly confronted with a wide range of life's physical, biochemical and mental-emotional stressors, adaptation can occur through the brain's neurohormonal *HPA axis* (hypothalamic-pituitary-adrenal). Music can help us better adapt by influencing this and other key chemicals like oxytocin, testosterone, the estrogens, prolactin, endorphins and endocannabinoids.

Music also activates the dopamine system, our brain's reward center. Dopamine is a hormone and neurotransmitter that influences movement, memory, motivation and pleasure, along with positive emotions and reward, a reason music can create such a relaxing euphoric state. Dopamine can be triggered by the *anticipation* of a rewarding event, perhaps as much or more than the event itself. Dopamine may also be a key reason music is such a powerful therapy, even for those with severe brain disorders such as Alzheimer's disease and other forms of dementia, helping them to retrieve memories and engage with the world when they previously could not. Dopamine is a positive reinforcement encouraging us to repeat pleasurable activities. (Cocaine, heroin, alcohol and other drugs can also influence dopamine to maintain negative addictions.)

Through these other factors, music can powerfully affect our states of consciousness.

Brain Waves

The brain normally changes consciousness based on what we're doing; or, what we're doing changes our consciousness. It's influenced by working, relaxing, mediating, listening to music or sleeping. Different states of consciousness are associated with specific brain waves, the electrical activity that can be measured clinically on an EEG. While not black and white, certain waves can occur in some areas of the brain and not in others. Here are four commonly measured brain waves:

- Beta. A busy active brain is a conscious state associated with the production of *beta* waves. These occur during internal or external chatter, discussing work-related activities, or giving or getting directions. While appropriate when needed, higher stress levels can keep us unnecessarily in beta, interfering with sleep, meditation or relaxation.
- Alpha. Creative consciousness is associated with *alpha* waves. Experienced when relaxing, deep breathing or meditating, alpha commonly occurs when listening to or playing music. In a healthy brain, just closing the eyes and reclining helps bring us into this loose, freely refreshing associative state of relaxed awareness. The more we *flow* into it, the easier it is to get and stay there at will — almost anywhere and anytime. This includes the potential to enlist the subconscious. Alpha can help balance stress hormones and the nervous system's tension-related sympathetic and relaxation-related parasympathetic components. A deeper alpha state could allow us to drift into theta.
- Theta. Children often live in their own private highly creative dream world in a state of consciousness associated with *theta* waves. Adults may experience

theta while falling to sleep — those cartoony dreamy wakeful thoughts often forgotten by morning (Paul McCartney described writing *Yellow Submarine* in this state). Theta can help us remember our dreams, connect to the subconscious, and improve long-term memory. Intense meditation or daydreaming can produce theta, a semi-lucid state of awareness decoupling us from our external environment while retaining powerful creative insight. They can appear in the transition to or from wakefulness or sleep, called *hypnagogia* (which can also evoke visual or auditory hallucinations, muscle jerks and sleep paralysis).

- Delta. This wave is associated with deep sleep, important for nighttime rest and recovery from the day, and for dreaming when our conscious and subconscious state may overlap. An unhealthy brain can drift into delta during the day, increasing sleepiness or literally putting the person to sleep. This can indicate a sleep disorder, a serious problem especially while working, driving or studying.

As we move from high alert beta to the more relaxed and creative alpha and theta, we can continue descending deeper toward the subconscious sleep condition of delta. Poor health, illness and disease can significantly impair alpha and theta, while both can foster the potential to be significantly creative and therapeutic. (As alpha and theta have similar mind-expanding potential, I include both when referencing alpha unless noted.)

Alpha

From the onset of history, the experience of alpha and the subconscious remain a major part of Eastern and Western philosophy and religion. Long before this, however, humans would have regularly used alpha as a natural strategy to expand the mind on the way to becoming a superspecies.

Scientists refer to the use of alpha in many ways, from an important method of therapy to the exploration of psychic reality. It can also be described as *free association* of what comes spontaneously to mind in a creative or therapeutic setting. (Alpha is also associated with the activities of numerous brain areas called the *default mode network*, or autopilot, discussed in a later chapter.)

In the 19th century Sir Francis Galton may have been the first to describe free association, a technique Sigmund Freud expanded upon, and later psychoanalyst James Strachey considered it the first scientific method to evaluate the mind. Free association is one way I describe songwriting: translating and transforming a feeling into music and lyrics. It's a form of improvisation, expressing without preconceived ideas.

In the 20th century, writer Virginia Woolf used alpha in her *stream of consciousness* approach to writing. Psychologist Mihály Csikszentmihályi coined the term *flow* in 1975 to describe this state of intense mental activity. Soon afterwards, Harvard professor Ellen Langer used the term *mind-*

fulness in very similar ways. Former Harvard professor Richard Alpert, aka Ram Dass, along with other 1960s counterculture individuals like former Stanford University professor Timothy Leary, promoted the use of psychedelics to achieve these states.

Music can increase these and other experiences significantly. While traditional meditation, classes or other mind-training disciplines can be important studies, they are steppingstones — ultimately, we should be able to always continue improving our brain anywhere, anytime. I developed the *Five-Minute Power Break*, described in Chapter 8, to help further encourage this endeavor through cultivating the alpha state.

5
The Indispensable

Just expanding your repertoire of active music listening is a simple and powerful action. It can quickly help expand the mind, and literally grow the brain for better performance. Music allows us to express our individual existence and creativity, whether in the form of simple awareness of ourselves, of others, or just to bring out the joys of life, regardless of whether we play, sing or listen. Music is as important a part of us as any other, and when turned on it has the power to improve us in almost unlimited ways. It's a form of biofeedback.

Brain vs. Mind

The word "brain" is used throughout this book with the understanding that each person's brain is uniquely their own. In short, the brain is our essential being. What about the "mind?" I define it similarly and say the mind is also the brain. In common and scientific literature, the terms are often interchangeable. In short, this three-pound high-fat electrical organ is our physical, biochemical and mental-emotional existence, conducting the body like an orchestra.

All creative expression comes out of the brain, enlisting its many components including intelligence and intuition, the conscious and subconscious, motor and rhythmic control, speech, auditory and visual centers, and emotions, including those used for the basic survival skills of instinctual thinking and behavior.

We begin expressing individuality even before birth through simple thoughts and movements. Give a young child almost anything, even the crudest items to play with, and some freedom, and what follows is often amazing creative expression, revealing a deep artistic dream world. As adults, uncovering the child within is a powerful form of creative expression.

Our brains also communicate with others, and music is one of the links. It's the emotion expressed by the person creating and that experienced by the listener. In a music video this expression is of greater intensity as more areas of the brain are engaged by the visual aspect. In a live performance, both the performer and audience are even more connected, acutely aware of each other's existence.

Early in my songwriting career, after being complimented on a new composition, a musician friend said that a great song almost requires a performance for others; only then would I truly understand the creation. With some initial reluctance, the experience helped me see and feel what other brains felt. It has been a valuable and potent part of the creative process ever since. It's like expressing love, it always comes with a response — good, bad or otherwise.

Listen to the Music

The first crucial component of expanding the mind through music is the simplest: listening. The brain takes in; the brain gives back. It's really one single action, a powerful loop that enlists us to act on music. As such, this is the first and most indispensable form of music biofeedback.

Regardless of your current level of listening, consider participating in three primary music lifestyle factors regularly to encourage substantial brain-body benefits. They include listening to oldies, to newbies, and participation.

- Listening to the music we love can enhance our daily lives. Virtually everyone has favorite songs, bands or composers. Let's call them *oldies* as they evoke key memories from our past, such as when first falling in love. They make us feel especially good — and younger. You probably remember at least some oldies, and by beginning this process others may come to mind. These are so powerful that someone with serious cognitive impairment may immediately become alert when hearing them. More benefits can be obtained with active listening as opposed to passively letting others choose, or as background music.

- Another source of music that lights up the brain uniquely is the surprise. Hearing a great song for the first time can trigger memories and feelings never experienced. Its power mimics the novel discoveries of our early life, which activated neuroplasticity, brain development and mind expansion. Let's call these musical pieces *newbies*. Some could become a new favorite, while others may not. Yet most will serve as a strong surprise. It's an endless supply of discovery.

- Expressing our own personas outwardly is a third way to expand the mind. This involves participating on some level during music listening. It can be as simple as tapping a foot or finger to a favorite tune, or dancing easy, moderately, or wildly. It could also involve singing along with a song or playing an instrument. Writing music is a powerful way too, even if you keep it a secret. Anything goes — singing in the car or shower, thinking or daydreaming about singing or playing, and just tapping a few notes on the piano as you walk by with a quiet hum. These are all powerful creative interactive expressions with the potential for quickly captivating the brain. As music is already within us, there are many ways to get it out, one note at a time.

These three simple listening processes can also create an intense alpha state, like meditation, to help build many new brain connections. Among the indications are feeling good, chills, powerful memories, tears or more.

Avoid various sources of stressful music from the Internet, TV, and radio (use the mute button), in stores and malls (listen to your own music with earbuds), and yes, even elevators (use the stairs). This is not the music most choose to hear. Instead, decide what music listening pleasure is important for you.

If needed, below are some specific music suggestions easily accessed online (oldies are not listed as only you can choose them).

Newbies include music you're not familiar with or never heard before. In addition to those recommended here, ask friends and family for their favorites. Listening with others, then discussing the feelings evoked by the music, can further help expand the mind. Venture out into unknown music genres you're not familiar with; from a classical piano piece to grunge punk rock; from Beethoven's "Moonlight Sonata" to Nirvana's "Smells Like Teen Spirit." All music is much more similar than not, composed of a relatively small number of notes — it's the individual's *response* that's different, with a desire to hear more of some or less of others. Regardless, even listening once is a significant enough experience, an experimentation, that can expand the mind. Here are a few suggestions:

- Beethoven's "Moonlight Sonata" is a powerful classical piano piece that's somber and wonderful.
- Among her many great love songs, Joni Mitchell's "Cactus Tree" withstands the test of time to still bring tears.

- Another great classic with the power of rhythm is "Take Five" by Dave Brubeck and Paul Desmond, one of the most famous jazz pieces (recorded in just two takes).
- Recorded with only violins, cellos, violas and vocals, the Beatles' "Eleanor Rigby" is a unique blend of classical and rock music.
- Dan Wilson's "Free Life" is a gem.
- You can also go to my website (MaffetoneMusic.com) for newbies as well.

An even more powerful way to enhance the brain's experience is through imagery. Music videos accomplish this extremely well, as do musical documentaries or movies that add storytelling, listening and learning. While music listening is a great way to replace TV-watching, music videos and movies can further enhance the benefits, especially as a healthy social event. Here are some:

- The '80s synth-pop band A-ha made one of the most all-time popular music videos (1.5 billion views), "Take on Me." Familiar or not, it's a potent mind-bending experience.
- The Avett Brothers, "No Hard Feelings." This simple effective video adds to the song's intensity.
- I wrote and recorded "Secret Lover" in Los Angeles, recently using it to make a dance music video.

Musical Diversity

A great way to combine oldies and newbies is by listening to demos of popular songs.

- Paul Simon's solo recording of "I am a Rock" (on his little-known 1965 album, the *Paul Simon Songbook*).
- Crosby, Stills and Nash released a whole album called *Demos* of their popular early songs.
- A powerful oldie/newbie video is George Harrison's demo of "While My Guitar Gently Weeps." The acoustic version is on the Beatles *Anthology*, with the video celebrated in a *Cirque Du Soleil* available online.

Sometimes, covers of songs by great artists can be powerful too. Neil Diamond's recording of Bob Dylan's "To Make You Feel My Love" and Johnny Cash's version of Trent Reznor's "Hurt" are stunning.

Learning about certain aspects of music, from how a song was written, to a unique feature of a certain genre, can greatly influence our appreciation. Studies show that people who strongly dislike a type of music like rap (or classical, or folk, etc.) find enjoyment of it after understanding more about the style. A documentary of Leonard Bernstein recording the music for the movie *West Side Story* with José Carreras and Marni Nixon is a fascinating example that could bring you to tears. Others include the movie *The Last Waltz* and the *Beatles Anthology*.

Your listening environment is important too. The best is being in a quiet location using earbuds, headphones or a high-fidelity sound system.

The Genre Game

The roots of our music sprouted from the start. Everyone sang their own unique songs, listened, responded, shared and benefited. This singing language of storytelling songs stimulated brain development, eventually encouraging societies, then verbal dialect, and ultimately a superspecies.

What do we call human music? The simplest and most accurate is folk, referring to everyone.

Of course, for millions of years human folks were also singer-songwriters. We make music of a creative purity, with natural, holistic and individual feelings, distinguishing us from each other.

Gradually, previous song influence and natural modification increased complexity. Instruments added more sounds, like simple flutes and striking of stones, the lithophone. Mathematics brought music theory expanding into Eastern then Western classical music. The diversity continued in every direction.

Both folk and singer-songwriter are among the many genres today.

Legendary musician Pete Seeger said that ordinary people create new songs from older ones to fit their personalities, and individual and community needs. A musical masterpiece ranging from classical and folk to dance and hymns is Aaron Copland's "Appalachian Spring," written for Martha Graham's ballet of the same name.

Singer-songwriters are passionate biologic biographers, emotional promoters of physical and mental music, reflecting an ever-expanding brain, sharing the essence of humanity moving forward, seeking more than mere survival, including peace and love.

While industry genres increased in the 1940s, today, including subgenres, there are hundreds. Like music grouped by decade, they play a marketing role for the industry, and media, while the risk for consumers is in restricting exposure to the full spectrum of music, which can limit the brain. Please expand your listening to all music, regardless of genre, whether recommended by family, friends, colleagues or this book.

Music can take us on a magical mystery tour to the center of the mind, exposing us to other worlds — accomplished simply through regular music exposure. While this chapter emphasized active listening, the next one expands this participation.

6

Embrace the Lazy Brain

Humans possess naturally lazy brains, and have from the earliest beginnings. This is fortunate, as it proved to be an important survival trait. In modern times it remains a key to helping expand the mind. Consider that we constantly strive to figure out better and faster ways to do more complex things, with less expenditure of energy. Perhaps it's just so we can spend more time hanging out under a shady tree in the cool summer air — which just happens to be how many great ideas originate. Let's embrace some important lazy strategies for more music benefits.

Our highly efficient brain only seems lazy, yet it's sad how harmful social stigmas can infect our behavior. A text from the 1500s suggesting we should *put our nose to the grindstone* was surely not meant to be taken literally. This was followed by Ben Franklin's *no pain no gain* mantra and came long before Jane Fonda's *more is better*. Actually, the notion of "less is best" is not laziness, but rather a great way to learn more music faster while having fun.

A healthy obsession for passion is what can prevent the common problem of burnout, poor learning, overtraining, or other brain-body breakdowns very common in virtually all fields, including music.

Case Study: She began piano lessons for the love of music. Hour-long weekly sessions were followed by repetitive daily practices. Seven years later — and still unable to play anything other than scales and easy songbook pieces — she quit out of frustration and developed a dislike of music.

The conclusion of this case is in the next chapter, but first there are important details about shortcuts in learning to play music. Here is an opportunity to play and create with purpose and pleasure, and, whether beginner or most gifted, improve while building a better brain and body.

To be effectively lazy we need to know the natural shortcuts. One we already possess is biofeedback.

Music is Biofeedback

Early human brains relied on their built-in neural system of biofeedback. It's defined as a natural mind-body mechanism with benefits that can improve physical and mental-emotional health. Like music, biofeedback is a natural capability all humans possess — an instinctive hardwiring for survival and adaptation. Early examples include sensing uncomfortable temperatures leading to the use of clothing, shelter and fire, and walking on rough surfaces leading to wearing protective footwear. Today, natural biofeedback remains essential for mind-body interactions — including the use of brain areas once thought not consciously controlled.

While usually considered separate, music and biofeedback both can influence the same biologic parts of us, a reason each can successfully treat the same health conditions. The nature of music and how we use it, including all the different approaches described in this book, employs natural biofeedback.

Clinically, I've used biofeedback from early in my career, developing approaches for heart-rate exercise monitoring, physiotherapy, stress regulation and others. Traditional biofeedback tools such as EMG (electromyographic) for muscles and EEG for the brain were incorporated and combined into manual versions utilized in assessment and therapy. This included the use of music listening *during* biofeedback.

An important music-biofeedback connection is both the conscious and subconscious synchronization of natural biorhythms to those in music, called *entrainment*. It's bidirectional: Music affects the brain to influence nerves and hormones, triggering muscles and movements that feed back to the brain. These effects are powerful even for those musically untrained.

Biofeedback also allows us to learn music in natural ways.

At some point in their lives, most people have played or sang at least some music — maybe minimally, or not for decades, but the experience is still in the brain for better or worse. While many millions have studied at least one instrument no matter how minimal, unfortunately most have given it up out of boredom, confusion, and the lack of fun and playfulness.

The act of learning itself can help promote creativity and build a better brain. So, learning more aspects of music, no matter your level even if you've never done it, is discussed in this book. It's much easier than you think.

Think about a young two-year old banging on the piano to create what is believed to be great music — it is, and they need a rousing applause (while parents practice restraint). Even a short single session is a powerful way to light up a child's brain. Adult brains work the same way. What separates good musicians from the great ones? A more creative brain. Regardless of where we are in relation to our musical capabilities, we can still progress further.

Learning Creative Shortcuts

We can benefit from shortcuts by enlisting our conscious and subconscious minds to learn. The brain uses the same neural networks for both, which have their own goals yet act like our behavioral assistants. (While best understood holistically as one, conscious and subconscious descriptions are often separated in this book for convenience.)

Most of our music, creativity, memory, learning, dreaming and other features exist in our subconsciousness, which, like sprouting seeds, enables us to consciously express our art. Continuously active, our subconscious is always learning and participating like autopilot in our daily activities, such as when performing a well-known piece of music, or while driving, so we can multitask without effort or focus.

One learning shortcut involves letting the brain be free to follow its passions, like the young child banging on the piano.

Learning itself promotes dual actions. We initially obtain brain-wide benefits, and afterwards learn what was initially intended. Just working on a short simple piano piece is therapeutic, then we learn the song. But without enjoyment it can be frustrating and unsuccessful. The story of Australian piano prodigy David Helfgott is another example of how traumatic early training almost destroyed his magnificent musical brain (as is loosely portrayed in the movie *Shine*).

We tend to learn too narrowly, at the insistence of others, without fun, or just enough to pass the test. Many only memorize the minimum basic chords of a song rather than the full complement of notes that make it so special. Beginning guitarists often learn a C chord, then F and G. Even on the piano this is a great beginning. While one could play many popular songs using these three chords, the brain naturally wants to keep learning, so don't stop it. Imagine if John Lennon stopped learning early on, or Mozart, Joni Mitchell, or any of the greats? Our brains are much more similar than not if only we keep learning. Passion drives learning to enlist conscious and subconscious shortcuts. It's like making dinner — we first prepare it, then put it in the oven for a while.

Incubate and Create

As a clinician, one of my first patients was a computer genius who helped develop some early industry breakthroughs. During the consultation, while seeking to uncover sources of work stress, I asked about a typical day. He would arrive and make coffee in the morning, then sit at the computer evaluating his ongoing research. After about 20-30 minutes he would start pacing back and forth in his lab, and often wander outside on the pleasant grounds of the facility. Only occasionally thinking about the computer work, he took in the sights and sounds of his surroundings allowing the brain to drift into a deep reflective, contemplating state, not unlike meditation. It might be an hour and a few sudden insightful "a-ha" moments before he was back to his computer. Soon afterwards, he was wandering the grounds again with the remainder of his day being very similar. My first thought after hearing this description was, *I'd like a job like that.*

My patient was encouraging the creative process to flourish by giving the brain, like a computer, the time and space necessary to process all the information. This is called *incubation*, a form of healthy mind-wandering or daydreaming. It encourages our subconscious mind to further empower creativity.

This natural shortcut is a type of rest period from the intense focus of a project, while searching for an answer, or trying to learn something. It's our autopilot we all drift into, a shift in consciousness when the brain produces more alpha waves. For this computer scientist, it was much more successful and efficient than sitting at the computer all day working on the same project, which may not let the brain freely wander, especially when interrupted by the physicality of keystrokes, auditory and visual inputs, and other potential interferences reducing success or even impairing the process. Many creative minds throughout history have followed very similar routines. In fact, years later Apple computer founder Steve Jobs became known as a prolific pacer.

When Lazy Minds Wander

Humans are known to mind-wander up to half our waking hours, with 2,000 mind-wandering episodes, give or take, in a typical day. Often interpreted as not paying attention or being interested, even as lazy or aloof, intentionality helps us wander in healthy ways. Pacing can be valuable too.

Pacing helps the brain intentionally incubate, a way to rest the mind while physically wandering. These rest periods away from the brain's intense focus function best when they are much longer than a focused work session, not unlike a music learning lesson. It can enhance creativity, learning, and memory while building a better brain.

There are two different kinds of mind-wandering associated with different states of consciousness:

- Intentional or controlled mind-wandering includes freely moving thoughts while not focused on a task. This healthy form was described above.
- Unintentional or unaware wandering can be unhealthy. It can occur when trying to focus or concentrate on a task but become disengaged from it. It can be induced by boring and unchallenged activities, by audio or visual distractions, and drugs or diet (by altered neurotransmitters). Mind-wandering during focused activities is abnormal, almost always distracting, and unintentional.

Our conscious intentions help us balance when to focus on performing a task and when to wander or incubate.

Music can help encourage healthy mind-wandering during non-focused tasks. This can support free-moving positive thoughts, especially in the form of images from music that can replace negative internal chatter. It works best when listening to the songs we choose. It's also not necessarily the music being played now, but the lasting lingering beneficial effects of previous listening.

Sometimes called a subconscious associative process, incubation can allow the subconscious to increase conscious creative thinking. But we don't always have to be awake. Sleeping also inspires creative insight and promotes better and faster learning.

When my health-related writing began to expand, I suddenly found myself pacing as well, also for longer periods than the time spent physically writing. Sometimes when returning to the desk it was like taking dictation from my brain. In the clinic, pacing between patients or while visiting one became essential to help uncover something unique that required time to further enhance the creative process. When I became a songwriter, pacing was a door to more musical learning and creativity, something that continues today.

The brain loves pacing. It increases its own oxygen-rich circulation, bringing in vital neural nutrients, sends out messages for muscle movement, with returning feedback creating a sort of neurostimulation. Much of our inspiration comes not with pen in hand or fingers on keys but feet on the floor.

In some art forms like Japanese calligraphy a deep alpha state of *mental pacing* precedes the physical creation. While it only takes a few seconds to express this beautiful character, it could take a prolonged period of preparation, as much time as necessary for the mind to enter a deep meditative enchanted state. Only then does the artist's brush stroke the paper.

Throughout history, creative explosions have often occurred not while hard at work but when daydreaming, showering, or upon awakening from sleep. Naturally lazy brains help link successful learning and creativity.

7
Learning, Playing and Plasticity

Whether novice or maestro, playing music offers more powerful benefits than just listening. Learning more of it is easier when starting at your individual level and expanding the mind to play better. This may seem obvious, but many people try to start at more advanced levels or use memorization instead of learning. These can limit and impair the brain. After achieving some level of ability, many are unable to further progress, playing in the same keys, chords, styles or routines. It's a form of brain injury that includes so-called *writer's block* among others. One remedy is enhancing creativity to continue where we left off making progress.

As children, we learn *play* for fun, although there is an important serious side. It's as vital a component of behavior as communication; play encourages brain-body development through plasticity. Playing music as adults extends this — it's the fun of bringing out our inner child. Just listen to the playful yet serious solo recording of "Blackbird" by Paul McCartney, who makes many sounds. He sings and plays a six-string guitar moving his right-hand fingers to position the chords while left-hand fingers are plucking, all the while he's tapping his boots alternately, keeping time.

Learning music is different than memorizing it. More cognition and creativity are enlisted through understanding, yet most learn music (and other things) using seemingly endless repetition of scales or chords called *rote* memorization. This is inefficient and reduces thinking and creating.

There is an important two-step process in learning music: a focused session, and a rest period. As explained, learning can be greatly enhanced not by more practice but less, with a turbo boost between sessions.

Staying more focused during practice sessions improves learning, especially when we understand the basic concept or idea (*I want to play the chords of this song*), visualize or imagine the movements and patterns (*watch my fingers make the notes*), and initially perform the movement *very* slowly (*as slowly as necessary to play accurately*).

Here are some important learning points to help grasp music faster and more efficiently:

- Shorter practice sessions followed by longer rest periods between them can be a highly effective way to learn. Even a single minute of practice, or a few short sessions spread throughout the whole day, can further enhance learning.
- Shorter practices can promote endurance, helping to prevent fatigue and improve performance.
- When practice sessions are longer, whether playing or singing, measurable performance plateaus occur

relatively soon, followed by decrements then by a reversal in benefits. This is due to neurological and muscular fatigue, even if we don't feel tired.

- In addition to impaired learning, longer practice sessions can reduce enjoyment, increase stress and increase the risk of overtraining or burnout.
- After practicing, resting allows the subconscious brain to keep imagining and reviewing the session.
- During rest, there is no need to consciously think about what was just practiced. It's preferable to focus on other things to allow subconscious information processing. Pacing can help.
- Compared to time spent practicing, more mental and physical gains can occur while resting. Taking this recovery time allows us to learn better and faster, and remember for longer periods, even after several days of no practice. (This is akin to the practice of mental imagery long used successfully by competitive athletes.)
- Similarly, classroom or internet learning can be more effective with shorter sessions and more breaks.
- The old saying *time flies when you're having fun* is appropriate. An indication that it's fun, effective, and therefore successful, is when time seems to pass faster. (Great songs do that too — they seem shorter than their actual running time.)

- Nighttime sleeping is important, too, especially during REM, which can amplify learning (called *overnight consolidation*). A short, quick review of your music practice in the evening can be a powerful routine.

Since our brains are uniquely individual, just how long, or short a session should last, and its rest interval, varies with your personal needs. Returning to the piano or guitar at the optimal time for another session is more about following the brain's instincts rather than timing the interval.

It's never too late to learn something new. Whether easy or difficult, passion often blurs the difference. While our bodies change more significantly as we age, a healthy active brain can keep learning to remain younger. What are your passions?

So, keep your piano open, take the guitar or other instrument out of the closet and keep it in sight. Any instrument will work, including your voice.

If you're starting new or starting up again, just play a note, any note; then two. Over a day or week, touch a key or pluck a string or two as you walk by — just make the connection again. These gestures may seem simple, and they are, but they trigger a powerful brain boost that could bring you to wonderful places. Or, if you are an excellent musician, learn another instrument, play a piano piece in the key of B, or expand in other ways.

One day I was listening to Ravel's "Boléro" when a neighbor came by to ask what I was playing. This young, hotshot hard-rock electric guitarist had never heard this great classical piece. I played it from the beginning, and he was mesmerized. After borrowing the record, two days later he asked me over to hear him play "Boléro," in all its complexities, on his electric guitar. I could almost see the new neural connections being made in his brain expanding his mind. It was as good or better than the 1966 version by Jeff Beck and Jimmy Page. Many years later, watching another great musician proficiently learn numerous Gershwin piano pieces on the guitar was also a treat.

Teaching Creativity?

Can we really teach creativity when already possessing it? Or does trying to force things risk impairing what naturally exists? It's best to encourage the brain to let the creative process flow. We often give children blank paper to draw or paint on, and it should be the same with music — and for all of us. There is always a blank canvas awaiting us to do with as we please, and certainly no right or wrong way to express creativity.

Expressing creativity is what humans have always done. But when we try to control, monitor or inhibit it — knowingly or not — we literally injure the brain's natural creative process. Sometimes this happens through our own beliefs. How sad that millions of people are quick to say they are not musical, believing it's not in their genes or brain when actually it's already in us all.

Then why won't our songs just flow out? They often do when not inhibited. Some people let it out by singing in secret, in the shower or car, during happy birthday or happy hour, or internally. Let's not hide one of the fun parts of music: letting it flow out. Enter improvisation.

Improvisation

So-called playing by ear without reading the notes or remembering a song is simply creating music free and natural by expressing our creativity. It's improvisation. In many ways, this oldest of human art today can be described as another effective shortcut.

Young children will improvise vocally, on the piano, or almost any other instrument, quite willingly when we let them. While it often appears bothersome to others, it's part of the process in any learning endeavor, and should be tolerated — it's how all great musicians began. Improv quickly lets the brain make the physical and mental connections with sounds.

Improv is not about randomly or just making up music but using more of the mind to increase creative expression. Paul Simon said, "Improvisation is too good to leave to chance." We eventually become less inhibited while the brain quiets our inner critic, further expanding the mind more than when reading music or playing something memorized. It may seem scary at first, but improv can significantly help improve and enhance us individually, and musically, and in other ways too — psychologists see it as a model to improve our world.

Improvisation can be done while playing on our own, singing solo without an instrument, called *a cappella*, and especially playing with others. No notes to read, and it need not be any specific song, just the natural unencumbered flowing brain.

Improv and songwriting can be considered the same — the music and words flow out. It's a form of free association (also used in talk therapy). All by itself, improv is like a separate special therapy that's also fun, the beginning of a beautiful relationship.

In the previous chapter, I started describing the case of the woman who took piano lessons for years but could not really play and quit with a dislike for music. There's a happy ending. After I quickly taught her a shortcut, described below, she first hesitated then suddenly could improvise with one of my songs, unfamiliar to her, with great joy and excitement. It brought tears to her eyes afterwards, because, as she stated, playing with others was what she always wanted to do.

Phil's Famous Three-Minute Keyboard Lesson

The response had often been disbelief, sometimes confusion, and occasionally anger. My now traditional three-minute lesson teaches all the basic major and minor chords and scales.

As a numerical concept, which spawned music theory, this is a great tool for anyone, including students and teachers at all levels. Rather than replacing music's intricacies, it's a steppingstone to help you start playing and enjoying right away. This simple model is one I stumbled upon that led to better songwriting and learning the complexities of music theory.

An immediate goal of this lesson is to be able to start playing more music on a keyboard right away. You might be able to improvise, pick out a melody, or even write an original song. You'll know 48 different scales and chords, 12 each for major and minor scales, plus major and minor chords.

If you're unfamiliar with a keyboard, please watch the short video of this lesson on my website for demonstration. For those a little familiar with a keyboard, this shortcut is briefly described below.

Most popular songs use chords, and in this lesson each chord has three notes. Each scale in this lesson has eight notes. I'll use the C major and minor chords and scales as examples and make suggestions for fingering but use those most comfortable for you. First, the chords:

Major Chords:
- First play the C note with your right thumb. Now count each piano key (white and black) to the right

1, 2, 3, landing on the fourth note (the E) playing it with your index finger. Now count right 1, 2, and land on the third key (the G note) playing it with your pinky. Now play all three notes at once. This is a C major chord, and the formula for finding all major chords is 43 (this one is C43). To play a B major chord, the formula is B43, etc.

- Now use your left hand to play the same chord on the lower octave to the left, starting with the pinky for the first note (C), then the second and third note.

- Using both hands, now play all six notes of the C chord.

Minor Chords:

- The routine is the same but has a different pattern — 34. Put your right thumb on the C note, then count right to the third key (Eb), then four more (G). This pattern is C34. All minor chords follow the same 34 pattern. Then use your left hand to play the same chord, using the pinky for the first note.

- Using both hands, now play all six notes of the Cm chord.

Here's a simple common chord progression: C F G. Many great songs have come from this pattern; after a verse of C F G, a chorus of F G C often follows. How about C Am F G?

Learning scales is just as easy.

Major Scales:

- First hit the C note with your right thumb. Count two to the right and play that key, then two again, then one, then two, then two, then two. Count one more and this last note is the octave of the first C. For the C major scale all the notes are white keys. This pattern is 221 2221. All major scales have the same pattern.

Minor Scales:

The routine is the same with a different pattern being 212 2221.

If you know the key for a particular song, improvise using the scale of the same key.

Another Important Shortcut

This has been mentioned before, yet it's one that too often eludes people. Humans have done it from the beginning without knowing anything about music, other than letting it flow out. Using the simplest musical know-how, one could more easily write an original song than learn someone else's. Many have done just that — like I did. It's not just mind-expanding but mind-blowing. And once you start you won't be able to stop. It might only require two chords to get started, not unlike some great songs from Led Zeppelin and Nirvana to Van Morrison and Bruce Springsteen.

These healthy shortcuts could very well quickly launch you into playing music, improvising, even expressing your own.

8

The Five-Minute Power Break

Combining music, deep breathing, relaxation and other activities can help bring us into a powerful alpha state quickly, as part of a whole brain-body healthy response. Don't underestimate the power of this five-minute routine. It's an intense musical meditation. I am continually amazed at the physical, biochemical and mental-emotional benefits it unlocks.

Other researchers have shown that five minutes of deep breathing can significantly improve the brain's cognition (mental activities associated with thinking, learning and memory), and behavior (our actions and reactions). In addition, the breathing cycle corresponds to that of the heart's; the results benefit the lungs, heart and blood vessels. Muscle activity increases, too, including the abdominals and various others positively affecting posture, movement and energy. Overall, this short simple session can help reduce stress, lower blood pressure, improve breathing, speaking and singing, reduce anxiety and depression, control pain, balance blood sugar and improve sleep. Through decreased oxidative stress and systemic inflammation, it can significantly and positively affect aging.

The benefits of the Five-Minute Power Break are similar to those obtained over time using both aerobic exercise training and meditation.

We don't always have time to exercise, take a class or meditate for long periods, but a five-minute break is possible for virtually everyone. It combines music with movement in a unique holistic way and one of my most potent self-care remedies.

Here's how to perform the Five-Minute Power Break:

1. Sit, recline, or lie down and relax.
2. Keep eyes closed and relaxed.
3. Position your hands or crossed arms at rest on your upper abdomen.
4. Using your diaphragm and abdominal muscles, breathe slowly, easily and deeply:
    - Inhale (preferably through the nose) for about 5-10 seconds with easy pushing out and relaxing of the belly. During the last 1-2 seconds of inhalation, add mild chest expansion — enough to feel contraction of the muscles in the upper chest, front shoulders and neck. (If you feel the need to yawn, let it happen.)
    - Exhale (preferably through the mouth) about 5-10 seconds. This involves contracting the abdominal muscles — pulling them

inward like they're trying to reach the lower spine. During the last 1-2 seconds, contract the pelvic floor muscles (like a Kegel exercise).
5. Listen to enjoyable music for about five minutes (headphones or earbuds are best).

Perform this activity daily, or more often if desired. Listening to one song or two shorter ones is better than using a timer. You can exceed five minutes if desired. When the music is less than five minutes, use the remaining time to enjoy the relaxed silent afterglow. The best songs are those with great alpha-wave potential like the oldie "Bridge Over Troubled Water" (Simon and Garfunkel) at 4:56, or some surprises: Lisa Hannigan's "I Don't Know" (4:56), my shorter "Rosemary," or in Berlioz's *Symphonie Fantastique*, the "Witches' Sabbath" (5:05).

With several mental and physical efforts at play during the Five-Minute Power Break, it could take some time before reaching a level of ease. If too challenging, try performing it with normal breathing, eventually incorporating full breaths.

Three muscular areas work in harmony during the Five-Minute Power Break — middle, top and bottom:

- Beginning with inhalation, the *middle* area involves the abdominal muscles relaxing so the belly pushes out allowing the diaphragm to contract and lower pulling air into the lungs.

- During deeper inhalation the *top* part enlists more muscles to contract including those between the ribs, front of the chest and neck. If yawning, jaw muscles contract too.
- Breathing out reverses these actions, and with deeper exhalation the *bottom* contracts through the abdominals and pelvic floor muscles.

Caution: If you start falling asleep, it means you're no longer in alpha but drifting into delta, which may indicate a sleep disorder. In this case, five minutes is too long — stop before drifting off. Even one or two minutes of alpha is healthy. Gradually work up to five minutes.

A sleep disorder could be due to a lack of sleep quality and quantity. We require seven to nine hours of healthy uninterrupted sleep each night — falling asleep relatively fast and staying there all night (should we wake, it's for a very short time while quickly returning to sleep).

Another common condition adversely affecting alpha is *carbohydrate intolerance* (*insulin resistance*) which can also impair sleep. It's most obvious when getting sleepy following a meal containing carbohydrates, especially one with added sugars, which can drive the brain into delta. (Other indications of carbohydrate intolerance include excess intestinal bloating and excess body fat, especially in the belly.) Eliminating refined carbohydrates and sugar and adjusting natural carbohydrates while monitoring symptoms is a very effective remedy and discussed later.

Other lifestyle factors that can prevent entering alpha include very high levels of stress from different sources that increase the hormone cortisol (causing people to wake during the night and be unable to quickly return to sleep). Certain muscle imbalances in the neck and head can also reduce or prevent us from entering alpha. These can result from chronic sitting, unresolved dental issues, whiplash, falls or other trauma.

Beyond Kegel

While Kegel exercises have been popular for decades, the Five-Minute power break enlists more pelvic floor, abdominal, chest and neck, and other related muscles that can lead to a better outcome.

For men and women, the Five-Minute Power Break can help the pelvic floor muscles, those making up the bottom or floor of the pelvis. When contracted, they lift upward, and are the same muscles used to stop the flow of urine mid-stream. Improving the pelvic floor can help prevent accidental urine leakage or passing gas or worse, and influence the uterus, prostate, bladder and bowel, especially if prolapsed, and all the pelvic structures while improving sexual sensitivity and function.

Weak pelvic floor muscles may be caused by trauma such as surgery (including prostate, abdominal, uterine, bladder), local pelvic injury, pregnancy and delivery, excess body fat, loss of fitness, and hormone imbalance. Other physical problems near the pelvis and abdomen, including hips, low back, and spine, can also impair pelvic floor muscles.

Yawning

As noted, if you feel the need to yawn during the Five-Minute Power Break, let it happen. This activates more muscles in the neck and around the TMJ (temporomandibular jaw joint). Yawning is a *pandiculation*, an involuntary brief contraction-relaxation of various muscles. This stimulates many brain areas, triggering neurotransmitters like dopamine and serotonin, and sex hormones. Many muscles are affected, along with ligaments, tendons and other soft tissues, and joints and bones, which influence posture, movement and balance. Yawning is like a mini full-body therapy.

Yawning does not infer boredom. While an evening yawn may precede sleep, in the morning or daytime it can increase oxygenation and attentiveness, arousing the brain.

For vocalists and others often using their voices, yawning helps open the glottis and better position or lower the larynx to minimize muscular effort when singing or speaking. This means the Five-Minute Power Break can be a great warmup to lessons, lectures and music performances.

Impaired or *deregulated* yawning occurs much more than normal, or little to not at all, which may indicate health problems. These may include excess stress and autonomic nervous system imbalance and can be associated with the autism spectrum or other brain injuries including Parkinson's disease. Yawning accompanied by pain often indicates muscle imbalance in the head and neck affecting the TMJ.

Because deep core muscles of the torso are contracted, this routine can be effective for those with *diastasis recti*, a common abdominal muscle weakness and separation of connecting tissue (the *linea alba*) occurring during and after pregnancy. This condition can cause the belly to stick out above and/or below the belly button, and contribute to low back, hip, pelvic, and other pain. The problem can also occur in men and women from excess body fat or exercise overtraining, especially weightlifting, sit-ups, and push-ups. It can be worsened with high-intensity or strenuous activities, and with deep inhalation breath-holding.

The Five-Minute Power Break, which I call *respiratory biofeedback* in my clinical presentations, is recommended before hands-on therapies as it can help balance muscles throughout the body. For everyone, successfully performing the Five-Minute Power Break can make it easier to reach alpha, helping the brain get there more on its own, further adding to feeling more refreshed, relaxed, balanced and younger.

9
Music Soothes the Aging Brain

We start aging from the moment we are born. This process continues even as we are improving our physical and mental capacities. By our 20s there are measurable reductions in physical abilities, and most people by age 40 experience measurable declines in mental function. Age-related cognitive decline is common, as John Prine's moving tribute to seniors "Hello in There" portrays. But it's not normal or necessary.

The fact is, we not only can postpone brain dysfunction, even while maintaining what's been built, but we can also *regain* what was lost along the way. It's possible to enhance brain function at any age. In doing so, we improve our quality of life.

Music's history is filled with those who continued recording and performing well into their 70s, 80s, 90s and beyond. They include Willie Nelson, Tony Bennet, Loretta Lynn, Paul McCartney, Bob Dylan, Dionne Warrick and many others including the Rolling Stones. At 81 years, Paul Simon's new album, *Seven Psalms*, is yet another incredible artistic breakthrough. Modern classical composer Elliott Carter continued writing prolifically until his death in 2012 at age 103.

While we can't stop *chronological* aging, we can influence *physiological* aging. The brain has the potential to continue being better until the end. The brain essentially can outlive the body. Through our lifestyle, we have much more control of important brain features, as mentioned in the Introduction. We can rewire the brain's cells, the vital part of successful brain aging, through neuroplasticity. We can even make new cells, through the process of neurogenesis, which the rest of the body does too.

A recent study demonstrated how lifestyle factors can help the brain function more like someone 20-plus years younger. These eight modifiable risk factors can significantly diminish brain function:

- Low education (not finishing high school).
- Hearing loss.
- Traumatic brain injury.
- Alcohol or other drug abuse.
- Hypertension.
- Cigarette smoking (currently or in the past four years).
- Diabetes.
- Depression.

Each factor led to a decrease in brain performance equal to three years of aging. A 70-year-old without any of these risk factors could, hypothetically, have the brain of a 46-year-old.

But we can do better and influence physiological age even sooner. Other risk factors appear long before serious health decrements. They include key components in the areas of nutrition, stress, physical activity, routinely expanding the mind, and regular exposure to music, as discussed in this book.

Despite decades-long increases in *life expectancy*, which actually has fallen since before the Covid-19 pandemic, all those years gained are at the end of life when the great majority of people are unhealthy. What good is a longer life if we can't enjoy it? Instead, we should focus on *health expectancy* as it is a factor we can influence considerably. Unfortunately, social trends about age continue to prevail. Even healthcare politics and scientists get confused.

Is Aging a Disease?

Some scientists want to call aging a disease. This in part is due to the notion that the process of aging fits the disease criteria of the World Health Organization's International Classification of Diseases. Also, it would allow more funding to study this "disease" called aging.

Just the concept of aging being a disease is enough to expect increasingly poor health. It could also further exacerbate the global endemic of ageism — age-related discrimination. And it maintains the myth of anti-aging hype connected with sales of products and services that don't work very well, if at all, and can be harmful.

Instead, let's refer to *healthspan* and *quality of life*. A healthy lifestyle that includes more music can significantly promote both. They can also address two very common impairments including mental-physical fatigue and brain injury.

Fighting Fatigue

Perhaps the most common complaint heard by clinicians is chronic fatigue. It is best defined generally as ongoing mental and physical fatigue, and sometimes the word exhaustion is more appropriate:

- Mental fatigue: Poor cognitive, emotional, behavioral, and other performance affecting daily life beyond memory, attention and mental processing.

- Physical fatigue: Poor strength, endurance and recovery, sometimes even from simple daily activities.

Mental and physical chronic fatigue can occur during aging and at any age. But despite being common and sometimes debilitating, the problem is not normal. Worse is that it is often unrecognized and therefore untreated. It can be secondary to disorders such as cancer, heart disease and stroke, but is often from imbalances in nutrition or physical activity. Medications can cause considerable mental and physical fatigue too, including drug interactions, especially when prescription or over-the-counter meds are excessive or unnecessary.

The good news is that through a healthier lifestyle, improved brain-body function can follow.

Brain Injury Spectrum

None of us have perfect brains. We all have some form of brain injury due to physical micro- or macro-trauma, minor or major biochemical toxicity, various levels of mental-emotional stressors, or, most often, combinations that accrue during our lives. Common signs and symptoms range from anxiety and depression to stuttering and stroke, and from Alzheimer's to Parkinson's Disease. Even ceasing to improve the brain — expanding the mind — such as no longer learning, losing passion, or being mentally and emotionally inactive, could be considered a form of brain injury.

However, many brain injuries are minor, ignored or go unnoticed, especially those associated with music.

Because music impacts virtually all the brain, any injury could reduce the ability to process music perception, execution, memory, and even reduce our ability to enjoy and benefit from it.

Fortunately, we possess an important repair and adaptation mechanism, plasticity, that helps the brain neurologically reorganize itself, a potential that remains throughout our entire lifespan.

We know why we listen to music, but another question is why some people don't or won't listen or avoid it altogether. Reasons include they don't enjoy it, can't participate in it, or are embarrassed by it due to a brain injury called *amusia*, associated with poor pitch perception and production, rhythm, and an inability to perceive, enjoy and express music.

Amusia

After hearing Rachmaninoff's magnificent *Piano Concerto No. 2*, a patient with amusia stated, "It is furious and deafening." Others perceive beautiful music as the sound of banging pots and pans together.

Usually, recognizing melody, musical memory, lyrics, emotion, and other functions all at once is complex and one wired early in life. It may only take one relatively minor brain injury for things to break down.

Like other brain injuries, amusia can come with different labels as it can affect various functions. This includes speaking (aphasia) and can be associated with dyslexia or other learning disabilities connected with vision, motor/muscle disorders, and ADHD (attention deficit hyperactivity disorder). Consider that 30 percent of adults with amusia have dyslexia and over 30 percent of dyslexic children are musically impaired.

Problems associated with amusia may also include:

- The inability to differentiate the feelings conveyed between major and minor, and consonant and dissonant, chords.

- The inability to sing, whistle or hum a tune, or play an instrument, is evident when muscle impairment is part of the injury.
- Some can't discriminate between tunes, familiar songs, or learn to read music.
- Even those with the same amusia diagnosis can possess significantly different clinical patterns.

Unlike traditional definitions, I describe amusia as a *spectrum disorder*, inferring everyone with this label is not the same, despite common musical impairments. Functional, milder forms of amusia would appear on one extreme of the spectrum, often not diagnosed, with the most severe at the opposite end. The injured brain may detect music well, but the information may not be organized or even reach consciousness.

Around 300 million people worldwide may have a form of amusia, although some scientists and clinicians suggest the numbers are much higher, with dramatic increases over the last 50 years. Most have normal hearing and speech with early exposure to music. Traditionally two classifications of amusia are *acquired* (occurring following birth) and *congenital* (before birth), but I will only use the term amusia here.

While amusia is sometimes called *tone deafness*, some individuals can sing proficiently, and those without a diagnosis could have poor pitch singing or temporarily develop it. For example, about 30 percent of 7-year-olds sing inaccurately; some improve while others don't. These problems can bring psychological stress from schoolmates and adults, potentially pushing them further away from musical enjoyment. It can also lead to monotonal speech, the lack of variations in pitch, affecting socialization and communication.

Amusia can coexist with another brain injury called *autism spectrum disorder*, often characterized by impaired social communications and interactions, repetitive behaviors, interests and activities, and abnormal auditory processing. While they occasionally have enhanced musical ability — some are even savants — most have an inability to process musical, linguistic, and/or emotional pitch.

Thanks to the potential of plasticity, music can help improve the lives of many individuals with brain injuries. A key is recognizing signs and/or symptoms that indicate a problem and provide a guide to monitor treatment effectiveness as discussed in the next chapter.

10
Rewire and Reorganize

Regardless of whether a not-so-typical brain has a label representing an impairment or not, just listening to familiar and new music is a powerful therapy. This chapter details others. Most people with brain injuries can still enjoy music, although they may miss some of the intricate details because the music may be perceived differently. Everyone, including great musicians, can still improve the brain, their musicality and quality of life.

Being aware of certain clues, signs or symptoms reflecting some level of brain injury, is important. This further helps individualize our personal needs — matching the right musical components can rewire or reorganize the brain: neuroplasticity.

Below are three common specific impairments accompanied by the relatively easy at-home forms of music biofeedback that can help improve the brain and expand the mind, leading to more enjoyment of and benefits from music.

Binding Music and Lyrics

For many listeners it seems simple yet understanding lyrics in music is a relatively complex cognitive task requiring significant brain activity. A surprising number of people are unable to accomplish this, incapable of hearing some or all lyrics in songs or misunderstanding the words themselves.

Most although not all professionally recorded lyrical music is mixed and edited carefully by sound engineers so that listeners can better hear the singer's words. The exceptions are some recordings where the vocals are at the same level of loudness as electric guitars, including bass, and heavy percussion.

The inability for the brain to bind lyrics with music is not uncommon and is amenable to treatment. While being able to hear lyrics again would be nice, this can also improve a vast cognitive mechanism that could help many other areas of the brain.

Unknowingly, I discovered this lyrical challenge and its treatment while in high school. It was frustrating that I could not hear the lyrics of most songs while many others could. Saving enough money to buy the Beatles' *Sgt. Pepper's* album, I noticed that the back cover had the lyrics for each song. As I read and listened at the same time, it was, thinking back on that activity, as if I could feel my neurons making connections for the first time. I played the album and read the lyrics many times. Eventually, it was surprising to start hearing lyrics of other songs as well, even from a car or transistor radio. It would be many years later when studying neurology that the reasons for this problem and its remedy presented here worked so well.

Most people already know if they can't hear lyrics well or at all. Here is a simple three-step remedy to address the problem:

- Find the lyrics to a song (most are online) and read them to yourself while listening. Do this a couple of times, then choose another song. Use relatively short listening sessions of one to three songs each over a period of a few days.

- After a week or so, test yourself by listening to some of the same songs without reading the lyrics. Then listen to songs you've not seen the lyrics to; if you perform better, listen to songs you've never heard before.

- Usually, it's possible to begin hearing lyrics in unfamiliar songs within days or weeks. Difficult cases may take longer. Continue this process as needed. Eventually, once the neurological connections are made and you regularly listen to music, there may be no need to continue this biofeedback.

Cerebellum Beat

The body is the brain's drumbeat, and the cerebellum the conductor. Music, timing and rhythmic movements are very much related. The cerebellum, located at the back of the brain, helps coordinate this complex process with other areas too, such as the motor cortex which sends messages through nerves to the body's muscles. Whether tapping toes, dancing or drumming, and virtually any activity, this natural innate rhythm-generating mechanism enables efficient performance. Movement and timing are as much a part of music as melody, harmony and storytelling.

Good cerebellar function is so important that just playing music more accurately on the rhythmic beat can make one sound like a better musician, even if other skills have not improved. Since the cerebellum is also connected to many brain-body areas, this biofeedback can be powerfully wide-reaching.

The inability to effectively maintain even a reasonably consistent musical tempo can carry over to other areas. Many appear uncoordinated, clumsy, or have irregular walking or running gaits. Most are not athletic, and if physically active are less proficient and more injury prone.

A simple approach called *marching* is used to address this cerebellar dysfunction. It requires a small handheld metronome (free apps for phones and other electronics can be downloaded from the Internet) that accurately sound each beat.

- Using a metronome, first evaluate your ability to walk or march in place to a beat. Start with a relatively slow 80 beats-per-minute (bpm) or less. Then try walking around the house to the same beat. Your feet should hit the floor right on the sound of the metronome. Body movement should be relaxed and smooth. If that seems easy, increase the tempo to 90, then 100 or 120 bpm. Each time you go faster, keep marching and moving to the beat.

- If this is not easy to do at any pace, or you go off beat after a minute or so while stationary or moving forward, perform the same activity as therapy. Spend time each day marching or walking to the beat. Start slow and easy, and comfortably work your way to faster paces. Just a few minutes is enough to start.

- Gradually increase the time while moving around the house or office (you can use earbuds). When safe, walk up and down stairs too, very helpful as more muscles and corresponding brain areas are activated.

- The effectiveness may be observed after one to three days — it will become much easier to keep the beat at all paces. Add longer periods of marching to test endurance. In difficult cases success may take longer. Athletes find this technique helpful during training to improve performance, gait, and reduce risk of injury.

- If you play music or sing, using a metronome can improve rhythm for a powerful performance boost.

- Use the metronome workout for weeks or months, if necessary, until the brain is comfortable and capable of keeping the beat very effectively on its own.

Simple Singing

A surprising number of people claim they can't sing. Some are embarrassed to even try, even when alone. It may feel odd to them. Many believe they are tone deaf, often speaking in monotone voices every day.

The fact is, virtually everyone can sing and hum. And it could be used as a powerful biofeedback approach for the brain. It can help control additional muscles to sing or hum with more variety in pitch and add tonal variation to speech. While musicians are better at identifying different notes than non-musicians, everyone can train the brain for better *pitch recognition*, helping to sing, hum, and even talk more proficiently. *And* it can expand the mind. That's what simple singing is about.

When I began singing it was not easy for me. Listening to a lot of Bob Dylan's rough early vocals was helpful. Later on, when good vocalists started singing my songs, it became apparent: While they sounded better, I could usually get the raw emotion of my own song across better than those with advanced vocal skills.

While we enjoy hearing certain musicians more than others, it's usually not just their voice. In popular music, most successful singer-songwriters are not considered great vocalists, yet they get the emotion of songs across in ways that "make the young girls cry," as Barry Manilow sang. Most important is to express your own vocals, not imitate anyone else's. That's what singer-songwriter Manilow does so well, saying "Sinatra is great. Judy [Garland] is great. Tony Bennett is great. I'm pretty good. But you can go far on pretty good if you work hard and pay attention." ("I Write the Songs" was actually written by the Beach Boys' Bruce Johnston.)

From folk and rock, to country, jazz and rap, popular songs don't usually include classical vocals. One exception is opera singers, who are specialized professionals trained extensively in music and theater, working hard to express the emotions of the great composers.

For all vocalists, a key to better singing is a better brain. Therapeutic singing not only helps the voice, it allows us to hear musical intricacies such as vocal harmonies and instruments. Pitch recognition is an especially powerful part of using your voice. (Vocal warmups including the Five-Minute Power Break and other easy activities, along with proper singing techniques and the avoidance of oversinging, are important too.)

The perception of being tone deaf or a poor vocalist usually begins early in life when the brain did not develop important connections. Often, singing and speech problems are related to poor vocal muscle function, reducing control of vocal range and flexibility. Poor brain function can also make us talk and sing more monotonally, sometimes worsened by a related social stigma.

Hearing our own recorded voice is particularly odd, but only to us. While talking we hear our voice differently from what's recorded. Normally, we hear two sounds, one from our mouth to ears. The second is a vibratory sense transmitted through our bones into the brain, which is not heard on a recording, making us sound so different to ourselves.

Speech and singing are different skills associated with overlapping brain areas, although the mechanics of both are very similar. Usually, talking occurs at lower and narrower ranges of frequencies with singing at higher and wider frequencies. Many people claim they can't sing well yet use variations in pitch in speech without realizing it, emphasizing certain words, or ending a question with a higher pitch. This awareness of pitch recognition, which is associated with both speech prosody and processing melodies and harmony in music, is a valuable component of simple singing.

In most singing lessons another person plays the notes that help guide the voice. However, I think it's important for you to combine this kinesthetic sense into simple singing. It involves playing different sounding notes on a tuned keyboard or a stringed instrument that can be plucked such as a guitar.

The process may feel odd or seem difficult at first, but improvements will be noticed relatively fast, sometimes after a couple of days or a week or two.

The time of each session should be relatively short not long, and you don't have to understand anything about music to be successful.

1. Begin by standing, preferably, directly in the middle and facing the sound of the music so both ears are a similar distance from the sound. Then, play a single note in the middle area of a keyboard or a middle string on a guitar; play the note several times slowly, holding the note for shorter, then longer, periods. After finding the note close the eyes to improve hearing, awareness, feel, and in creating a mental image of the note. Some may even sense an associated color. Relax and focus on the note's sound and image. Meditate on the note. Take all the time you need to do this part, even if it makes up what you deem as a whole session. (If you're having trouble, try a different instrument if available or move to a different area of the keyboard.)

2. Now choose another note and continue as above, focusing, feeling, imagining what you hear. Proceed to another note if you feel ready. A few notes in total may be enough for the first session, even though you're not singing yet. This short stimulation can be the start of a very effective therapy — your brain will now take time to respond. You can perform the same short lesson later in the day if desired.

3. At some point, especially with closed eyes, your brain may naturally be making connections to muscles to replicate a particular note using your voice. Encourage this, perhaps by starting with a quiet hum. Use shorter notes first, then longer ones. Try

matching the sound made by the instrument. Over time as this becomes more comfortable, progress to opening your mouth and vocalizing using the sounds *ah* or *ooh*, or any sounds you are comfortable making regardless of quality or volume. Don't force it and stay relaxed.

4. Continue using your voice with other single notes. Avoid notes that are too high or low or difficult to vocalize — when in doubt or uncomfortable, choose another note.

5. As an option, at any point, especially if you have trouble hearing the differences between some notes, open your eyes and enlist vision: Look at the keyboard or string while playing the note several times. See the key or string make the sound. Now hit any other key and look at it while listening. Do this a few times. Continue adding other notes. Combine both vision and hearing of notes, especially the differences between two notes. Then hum.

6. Eventually, whether a day or a week, when you can better recognize and reproduce single notes, a more advanced progression is playing any two notes together at the same time. But without singing or humming. Choose from some notes you played previously. First use notes farther apart from each other, which are easier to distinguish than those closer together. Once this is accomplished, try distinguishing between two notes closer together. Use

shorter sessions, and a few times a day if comfortable.

7. Continuing a more advanced approach involves humming or vocalizing one single note while playing two different notes together.

Eventually, you may want to hum or sing along while listening to songs, or even make up your own music — using simple single notes. In addition to listening to both favorite and new music, simple singing can be complemented with other biofeedback strategies, especially binding of music while singing the lyrics. If needed, marching can help your timing of playing and singing. These and other suggestions in this book will keep your brain happy and busily expanding.

11
It's a Jungle Out There

It seems so simple, and it can be. Expanding musical horizons can improve physical and mental health and how well we age. For this to happen we must hear the happy sounds, even visualize them. With virtually all the brain influenced by music, it's no surprise its clinical use is extensive, from helping with minor health problems to surgery and intensive care, and for psychiatric illnesses like depression, anxiety, schizophrenia and others. There is still much for us to learn. For example, even the pitch of a guitar can influence the brain. In the 1930s, musicians began tuning instruments to a 440 hertz frequency instead of the traditional 432. Many are returning to the original 432, and studies show it offers more health benefits and less stress compared to 440.

However, in today's busy world it's important to tread lightly through a dangerous jungle that influences whether we benefit from music's wonders. Things like hearing problems, noise and junk music can have the opposite effect. Let's explore more of the wondrous ways music can impact the brain.

Making Auditory Sense

Hearing music begins as vibrating sound waves traversing the ear canals. Hair cells transform them into electrical signals, enhancing the frequency, transmitting them to the brain's hearing centers where we sense music. We also process sound *vibrations* that are conducted through bones into the brain, where things really start getting interesting. Musical sensations diffuse throughout the brain with some amazing effects:

- The limbic system illuminates emotion and memory.
- Visual areas trigger mental images (even if visually impaired) for memory, planning and decision-making.
- Our autonomic nervous system invigorates (sympathetic) or relaxes (parasympathetic).
- The cerebellum runs rhythm, sending motor messaging to the muscles and generating movement (imagining music can also do this).
- Dopamine, endorphins and other neurochemicals are stimulated, promoting growth, cellular repair and good vibes.

Mirroring Music

An infant watches people move, helping develop the means to eventually mimic activities of others. Unique brain cells called *mirror neurons* assist in this process. We use them as adults to sing, dance, learn or dream about it. Watching, even imagining, our fingers playing music may be powerful, beyond traditional learning alone. Seeing someone's right hand play can help guide both our hands. These are just a few astonishing examples of mind-expanding neuroplasticity.

Mirror neurons can also aid in:

- Creativity, empathy and other social-behavioral interaction and cooperation.
- Coupling melody, rhythm and other elements with vision to communicate meaning, emotion and memory.
- Encouraging listeners to see themselves in songs, or to imagine stories while listening to music without lyrics.
- Linking live performers with individual listeners, increasing awareness of each other's perspective.
- Self-awareness.

Mirror neurons could be why music can help those with autism, schizophrenia and other brain injuries. Imagine. Thinking about music can affect us like hearing it.

Impaired Hearing

An increasingly noisy world exposes potential hearing damage to billions of people, with a third of those over 65 already having hearing loss. Many others do too. It drastically impairs music listening, impacting physical and mental-emotional health.

Most hearing loss is preventable, with excess noise the most common cause. It can be temporary or permanent, impairing attention, language, learning and psychosocial wellbeing. This brain injury can increase the risk of dyslexia and ADHD, and trigger tinnitus, which in turn can promote depression, cognitive decline, dementia and even poor heart health.

Two common forms of impaired hearing include:

- Sensorineural, the most prevalent permanent hearing loss especially over age 60. Poor health increases the risk, including hypertension, heart disease, diabetes, iron deficiency, tobacco use and various medications like aspirin and antibiotics.

- Conductive hearing loss occurs from overproduction and/or impaction of ear wax. This is easy to diagnose and treat.

The dBs

External sound is measured by the decibel, or dB. A whisper is about 30 dB, normal conversation 50 to 60, and a motorcycle about 95.

Mental-emotional performance is influenced by noise beginning about 50 dB, while speech interference and annoyance can appear at 55 outside and 45 indoor. Noise at 70 can affect mood and if maintained can damage hearing. Many are routinely exposed to sounds over 100 — those above 120 can cause immediate damage. The average noise at entertainment venues exceeds 110. In the comfort of your home, moderate music levels are typically around 60.

Common noisemakers:

- Clothes or dishwasher, vacuum, loud talking, barking dog — 70 dB
- Lawn mowers, leaf blowers, city traffic from inside a car — 85 dB
- Subway, city traffic, car horn, sports stadium, power tools — 100 dB
- Higher-volume earbuds, phone, radio, stereo, and TV, close shouting or dog bark, music concert — 110 dB
- Siren, factory equipment — 120 dB
- Gunshot, firecracker — 140 dB

Loud noise stress can harm everyone (a reason high dB is sometimes used in torture). Individuals can monitor sound through a free CDC-recommended app (www.cdc.gov/niosh/topics/noise/app.html).

Ear protection, known to improve mental performance including reduced errors in loud environments, includes *ear plugs* (outer ear canal) for lower frequencies, and *earmuffs* (covering the entire ear) for higher. Each reduces noise by about 30 dB.

Noise stress can accumulate. Lower levels over longer periods are like short term louder volumes. Throughout life, exposure increases the risk of later hearing loss.

Managing our environment helps us hear more pleasurable sounds while avoiding harmful ones. Consider using clothes and dishwashers while away or at night if far enough from bedrooms, turn down or mute radio, TV, and Internet, reduce frequency of lawn care, and use ear protection as needed.

Noise Sensitivity

The opposite of music to our ears is unwanted noise. For many, even safe levels are intrusive, inducing physical and mental-emotional stress. How well the brain adapts to that intrusion determines our sensitivity. We all hear annoying sounds, but some people are more sensitive, reactive, and adapt slower based on the level of arousal. While noise sensitivity is not due to hearing loss, its tolerance ranges from extreme sensitivity to those who are noise resistant.

Those who are sound sensitive appear to be more intelligent and creative. Up to 40 percent of people are noise-sensitive, responding more startledly, not reacting well, and less able to ignore or block out unwanted sound. Also:

- Even when accustomed to noise many people have increased rates of human error associated with memory, attention, learning and reading.

- Noise sensitivity may correlate with mental health symptoms in autism, depression, schizophrenia and other brain injuries.

- Even moderate levels can induce a sense of inadequacy, depression, anxiety, sensitivity, anger, tension, inferiority, nervousness, physical and mental exhaustion, withdrawal, feelings of helplessness and distress.
- Noise sensitivity may be more common in quieter, introverted personalities.

Noise can interfere with the sounds we love and disturb our need for quiet. Einstein said everything in our world is energy, influencing us in ways that range from benign to violent. All sound has the power to potentially help and hurt us personally and as a society.

Beware: Weaponized Music

Sound, noise and music have long been used in the dangerous art of deception to encourage people to do and buy things that are unhealthy or unneeded. From business and politics, to media and entertainment, I call it weaponized music because of its strong connection to violence and war.

Studies show that violent music, even when funny, can increase aggression, hostile antagonistic emotions and aberrant behavior. It begins in children learning about war enhanced by music. Fighting, shooting and pretend killing use the good-bad clash to help rationalize violence. The music in video games, TV, cartoons, movies and online media further helps drive messages into the brain.

Aggression is global. In 2021, conflicts included 174 nations at war or in conflict, with only 23 countries living in peace. War, hostility, and aggression are glorified in society with martial or military music playing key roles. A long history of powerful emotional music and lyrics conveys strong political statements, a backbeat of marching songs, unification rallies and parades portraying glory. Classical music too — Tchaikovsky's "1812 Overture" conveys it without lyrics. Likewise, national anthems. Written in 1812, the U.S. "Star-Spangled Banner" contains aggressive music and lyrics. No doubt even the earliest battles between humans were driven by strong emotional music.

While there are many pro-war songs in country, rock, hip-hop and other popular music, there is also a long history of anti-war songs: Neil Young's "Ohio," Dylan's "Masters of War," Kate Bush's "Army Dreamers," and my own "Marches."

Certain components help weaponize music to trigger stress and aggressive behavior:

- Volume. Excessively loud music can cause brain-body hormone and neurological imbalance.
- Lyrics with aggressive words.
- Tempo. Fast-paced driving music (like at the gym) could rev up the nervous system and heart rate.

We certainly don't want to ban music, nor books or movies. However, when the risk of violence increases, rational assessment is in order. Prevention is proactive, much preferred and more effective than waiting for a traumatic event like a school shooting before reacting to it.

Weaponized music is just part of the accumulating buildup of unnecessary or low-quality music blaring out from our increasingly busy frantic world.

Junk Music

Sensitive or not, we must navigate a maze of noise pollution. It's a jungle out there. Whether loud, weaponized or obnoxious, junk music is synonymous with annoying noise, worsening sensitivity, contributing to hearing loss and adding to overall brain-body stress. It's like omnipresent junk food, except we hear it.

Along with pleasure, great song staying power appears when music-memory *hooks* grab us to sing along to ourselves or out loud with a repeated chorus. But advertisers have long used this specific feature for their advantage. They're called *earworms*, clips of carefully composed ads playing repeatedly in our minds and difficult to avoid or turn off. They also elicit involuntary imagery, so marketers double their pleasure.

Most people experience earworms, often finding a song disturbing, distracting and even an obstacle to thinking. Minimally, they disrupt our inner peace.

I sometimes refer to this audible junk as *monkey music* — commercialized, politicized, even industry songs quickly fabricated by focus groups. The name comes from the made-for-TV *Monkees* show, which features a group of actors obviously fashioned to mimic the Beatles. Monkey music is potent: We hear it and do it, buy without thinking. It's infectious — once we get an earworm it stays and plays in our head over and over.

Catchy earworms don't just compete for our brain's perception, emotion, memory, spontaneous thought and creativity, they're driven into long-term memory like malware. Like junk food replacing healthy food, earworms replace the music we love, whether thinking or hearing it. What's worse is the worms show up more during stress. The obsessive, repetitive compulsive nature of earworms adds to their success — trying to resist them with thought-suppression is futile, often making them worse.

Earworm ad jingles are bad enough. Other stress includes jarring alarm clock music, radio and TV commercials, annoying noises from the Internet, phones, and elsewhere. We hear junk music — known to promote negative thoughts — while on hold and in elevators.

The best approach is prevention — avoid the junk and choose the music we love. Fortunately, most junk music is relatively easy to mute or turn off. Now we can hear a love song's lyrics, the intricate instrumentals of a symphony, and the sophisticated sound of a beautiful solo. Or silence.

When was the last time you experienced real peace and quiet, sensing only the subtle sounds of your body? As wonderful as music is, silence is golden. One of my favorite sound memories was atop a 14,000-foot Colorado mountain: Feeling the vibration of each heartbeat, I heard the passing clouds.

12

Our Musical Personalities

Many people wish to change their personality traits. In the U.S. people spend more than $10 billion annually on self-help books and programs targeting this change. It's easier said than done. However, substantial research pairs traditional traits with music preferences. It appears there's a simple and pleasurable solution for broadening and improving the personality.

Studies show that almost everyone wants to change their personality traits to improve social and personal relationships, decision-making, and mental and physical health. These traits go far beyond extrovert and introvert first introduced by psychologist Carl Jung a century ago. Further categorizations, ranging from the *Big Five* traditional personality domains described below to the 16 Myers-Briggs types, are commonly used today.

We all have certain musical likes and personality traits that influence each other. This is our music personality, referred to here as *musicality*. Choosing to modify our personality is almost as easy as turning the dial or changing our tunes. Personality is strongly influenced by people and the environment. Experimenting with musical experiences to expand the mind can help keep our better attributes while allowing us to let go of others.

Experiment, Experience, Expand

Personality change is not about switching from being introvert to extravert or vice versa. We don't want to give up our individuality to become someone else. Instead, we want to be more of who we really are, extending our musicality and personality to expand our life experience. To paraphrase Joni Mitchell, we listen to music that others write to see ourselves in it.

Music influences us holistically by promoting a wide range of healthy physical, biochemical and mental-emotional responses. These brain-body interactions affect muscles, movement and energy levels, which in turn influence mood, memory and our very being. Studies show that feelings of happiness and nostalgia are more common during musical activities, while anger, boredom and anxiety take over during non-musical ones.

To literally help create new neural connections for a better brain, I designed a *musicality model* to guide us on an amazing journey of transformation. Experimenting, experiencing and expanding our musicality brings our whole being along for the ride.

The Music of Balance

The musicality model incorporates an important concept of balance, a theme that runs throughout this book.

While never perfect, we can continue striving for better brain balance using music to promote healthy cognitive, behavioral and personality changes. Balance is exemplified in the extraversion trait best seen as a spectrum from highly extroverted to highly introverted. Those in the middle, called *ambiverts*, are considered to have better personality balance.

Throughout my clinical, scientific and music career I've described balance as optimal physical, biochemical, and mental-emotional health and fitness. A yin-yang model might depict it as stability and change; each precedes and follows the other. We want stability in life and healthy change helps create it. Music and change are often linked. The groundswell of dramatic global social changes that peaked in the 1960s corresponded with equally great and broad changes in music. We naturally crave and strive for stability and change despite the challenge of achieving better balance.

Traditional Personality Traits

Descriptions of personality traits date back thousands of years in the writings of Plato, Aristotle, Hippocrates and others. Sigmund Freud greatly expanded these definitions over a century ago. Today's extensive research, scientific debate and detailed descriptions have categorized hundreds of traits.

Five commonly described traditional personalities are highlighted below. Most people don't fit into any single trait but rather a combination of two or more:

- Openness: intellectual, cognitive, creative, focused, curious.
- Conscientiousness: orderly, responsible, dependable.
- Agreeableness: good-natured, cooperative, trustful.
- Extraversion: extraverted, optimistic, sociable, talkative, assertive.
- Neuroticism: anxious, sad, negative emotions, strong reaction to stress.

These traits and other factors are used in the musicality model to help guide our journey of discovery and change. Also included are brain injuries, especially amusia, which influence personality.

The Musicality Model

As a self-care tool for use at your own pace, the musicality model can help us regardless of the starting point. By rediscovering oldies, experimenting with new music and increasing mental imagery, we can multiply our memories, surprises and alpha experiences to expand personality.

The model is divided into four categories:

- The two on top represent potentially healthier personalities.

- The lower two areas are associated with increased brain dysfunction.

An important goal is encountering and confronting more music outside our current personalities. It's important to experiment and experience more activities in the top two categories, even dipping into the musically limited moods.

As a non-dancer, writing dance music helped me break through to the other side. Other horizons opened with a simple *folk rap* song and performing in crowded hazy bars. Similar experiences expanded my mind farther out of its comfort zone into more strange and wonderful worlds — even those not needing an encore offered added value.

Our brain is not only naturally wired for music, but also for fear. Yet most of us have ventured into this unknown for success, learning we're also wired to manage uncertainty. Like music, expanding the mind has no rules or boundaries, potentially influencing us personally and socially by improving mental and physical health, and our world. Let's begin.

First, read through the musicality model as follows, see where you might be. Then choose the suggestions afterwards that apply to you. And don't be afraid to come up with your own.

Music Personalities	Features
Musically Expansive (Openness)	**Characteristics:** Feels music in a cognitive, creative, analytical, intellectual, inspirational, upfront/personal way. Attracted to music composition and all arts. Less extrovert, more introvert. Noise-sensitive. May use self-care. Easily moves into alpha. **Music:** Vast, reflective, complex; from folk and jazz to blues, rock, rap and classical. Carefully selective. Attracted to analog, avoids party, dance and popular radio music. **Listening:** High fidelity sound; softer moderate volumes.
Musically Comfortable (Agreeableness, Conscientiousness)	**Characteristics:** Balances stimulating/relaxing music often in background while exercising, socializing, driving, working. More extrovert, less introvert. Noise tolerant. Self-care likely. More beta/some alpha. **Music:** Popular, upbeat, rhythmic; soundtrack, soul, funk, electronic. Sensitive to musical needs of others. Enjoys larger music venues, dancing. **Listening:** Earbuds, smaller speakers, moderate to louder volumes.
Musically Limited (Neuroticism)	**Characteristics:** Uses music to sustain moods. Strong reaction to noise/stress. Risk of poor physical health. Experiences anxiety, anger, depression, feels self-conscious. Self-care less likely. More beta/little alpha. **Music:** Very narrow choices; intense and rebellious reinforcing negative emotion and mood arousal. **Listening:** Earbuds, small speakers, louder volumes.
Musically Injured (Amusia)	**Characteristics:** Can overlap with dyslexia, other learning disabilities despite good intellect; difficulty tapping a beat. **Music:** Indifference, often avoids, feels uncomfortable or annoyed. Social stigma of tone deafness, monotonal speech, and poor music memory. **Prognosis:** Potential for enjoying and benefiting from music. Considered treatable.

Start simple: break out of your comfort zone, even with a song or two. Use musical features from other categories not typical or comfortable for you. Venture into other musical personalities:

- Seek out newbies that are favorites of family, friends and others.

- Read about different, unfamiliar musical genres like a violin concerto, rap or jazz. Then listen to some.

- Experiment with new music that's intense, rebellious, or has negative emotion for mood arousal.
- Those more extroverted can spend more quiet time, such as performing The Five-Minute Power Break, or silence by muting music while working, driving, or exercising.
- Introverts can experiment with randomly selected songs, or the latest top-40, and perform marching with others, or dance.
- Those in the lower two categories can journey upward.

Certainly, songs that are uncomfortable, annoying or offensive need not be heard again. Listening once is a powerful learning experience for the brain. We might even uncover what's thought to be unlikely common features between the likes of Metallica and Mozart, or folk and rap.

For Musicians

- Learn a jazz version of a classical piece, happy birthday in a minor key, or by transposing your usual songs into difficult keys (without a guitar capo).
- Use improvisation with yourself and others.
- Learn and incorporate chord inversions.
- Play with a metronome, jam with others, go to an open mic.

Novice or not, writing your own song can be easier than learning someone else's. It won't be judged like the original, it will be yours alone. Yvon Chouinard (cofounder of Patagonia) said he "learned at an early age that it's better to invent your own game; then you can always be a winner."

We all have a story, real or make-believe. Writing *and* sharing it can greatly expand the mind, and personality.

The Alpha Club

Like talk therapy, music can bring great benefits in a group. As a teenager, getting together with friends usually involved playing records, from a new album and old favorites to mix and match. I looked forward to these events — quiet listening followed by passionate musical analysis. I call it the *alpha club*. Continuing through the years it dwindled as people got busy and habitual. I often recommend others recreate it. Sometimes I incorporate similar activities during my *music and the brain* presentations. An alpha club can be an amazing mind-expanding event.

Professional support can also be valuable in expanding musicality, whether a music or talk therapist, or others.

Covid Personality Changes

Significant population-wide changes in personality are rare but that's just what rapidly happened during the

Covid-19 pandemic. In the beginning, researchers found people more cooperative, supporting each other for the collective good despite isolation. However, sudden population-wide personality changes followed in the next year, including open hostility and social upheaval. A major decline in extraversion, openness, agreeableness and conscientiousness impaired our personal and social situations, trust, creativity and responsibility. Neuroticism increased, with risky behavior and poor mental health, especially in normally resilient younger adults.

Researchers equated these changes to those occurring over a decade of life. Seen across race and education, they can have major long-term individual and social impacts. Music could help.

Music plays a major role in expanding the mind for a better, more balanced existence — from the earliest moments of life to its very end. This can even occur when starting at the bottom and working up the musicality model. I am a case in point, spending my early years with amusia and other brain injury. Through adolescence and adulthood, experiences and experimentations helped my brain evolve and expand. Living through the extremes helped me to understand balance, which I continue striving for today.

13

Once Upon a Time: Beyond Storytelling

The story of a librarian's 1958 interview with Albert Einstein is posted on a Library of Congress webpage. She asked him what her child should read to improve intelligence. Einstein recommended stories. His suggestion was "fairy tales and more fairy tales." When the mother asked for a serious answer, Einstein added that creative imagination is the essential element in the intellectual equipment of the true scientist, and that fairy tales are the childhood stimulus of this quality.

People of all ages use stories regularly to reach each other. It's also a valuable part of our internal silent dialogue. Certainly, most of our night and day dreams are stories. Like our brain creating storylines when hearing music without lyrics. Dance, videos, and especially live performances, also invoke stories. While the best ones engage all our senses, when combined with music it solidifies them. Storytelling songs can further rock the brain to expand the mind.

We all have a story to tell because we're all part of the human story. Like music, storytelling itself can profoundly light up the brain. The earliest humans conveyed them long before language was developed. Words, of course, are not necessary to express feelings.

A Storytelling Story

Body language that included facial expressions, posture and gait, and vocalizations like humming and singing, even moments of silence, were used for communication between early humans. This would imply that the kind of simple songs our ancestors used and benefited from were the earliest form of storytelling music. Even in its most basic forms, conveying a story is a powerful artistic practice for communication and understanding. This is not a uniquely human trait — consider that even bacteria and plants extract information from their environment and successfully communicate it to others.

While music and storytelling are a natural match, we carry both in our brains most of the time, the reason we can create a story when hearing even a simple melody, and vice versa. This is another reason why writing our own songs is relatively simple — they're already there.

Certainly, reading poetry is a story, and usually comes with tonality, rhythmicity, and silent pauses, enlisting the musicality of the brain. Other special features of storytelling include:

- Music without lyrics can tell a story, just as storytelling without words creates imagery in our brains. Studies show the perceptions in the brains of listeners, who often report stories remarkably consistent with the composers of the music.

- At the same time, like songs, stories can be interpreted similarly or very differently by individuals.

- Paired with music or not, storytelling is a great form of communication linking performer and listener through the brain's mirror neurons. It's one reason live performances are such a powerful brain boost.

- While all animals experience the *here and now*, humans have the unique ability to also share stories of the past and future.

- People of all ages are fascinated by audible stories, including very young children even if they are unable to understand the words. Storytelling, like music, can bring out our inner child.

- Stories can communicate complex ideas in simple ways. Many storytelling songs can express the complex topic of love very effectively in two minutes.

- The power of storytelling is used in business to persuade people to buy, and by politicians and media for deception. Combined with the subconscious mood-altering effects of music it can mesmerize a population — the brain usually relies on emotion over intellect in decision-making.

Author Jonathan Gottschall (*The Storytelling Animal*) wrote: "We are, as a species, addicted to story. Even when the body goes to sleep, the mind stays up all night, telling itself stories."

While a story or song itself can grab the brain's attention, *introducing* it with another story can double the power. The story about the storytelling song might describe how you wrote it, reference the lyrics, or other personal aspects of the song drawing the audience in.

Storytelling not only evokes healthy changes within the brain, but it can also help people make special connections with each other, even strangers. It can merge a deep emotional experience between teller and listener — their alpha brain waves can even synchronize. Enlisting auditory and visual stimuli heightens our senses, allowing hormones to spark memories, emotions and empathy from start to finish. These are key reasons music is used in movies, advertising, retail settings and in other places where strong mental and emotional connections can be made. Music videos became so popular because they can drive the storytelling song better than the audio-only version.

Before becoming a songwriter, I was a clinician, where my storytelling skills were honed to better communicate with patients. In my health-related books, the many stories of patient and athlete experiences were very popular. And when lecturing and performing research, stories helped explain complex processes for practitioners and scientists.

Albert Einstein: Storyteller and Musician

In a 1929 *Saturday Evening Post* article, Einstein stated, "I am enough of the artist to draw freely upon my imagination. Imagination is more important than knowledge. Knowledge is limited. Imagination encircles the world."

Einstein was a wonderful storyteller who could imagine and write about concepts never told. The beginning of his scientific papers provides a wonderful storyline. Not being a physicist, I get lost in the later technical aspects of Einstein's papers, but the introduction is fascinating, evokes feeling and imagery of a complex subject I might never grasp otherwise. This process helped me develop the confidence and creativity to write on my clinical topics.

Balancing his life with music, Einstein said if he were not a physicist, he'd be a musician. He played the violin, and although admittedly did not do so very well, he loved playing classical music regularly with better players. He thought of abstract science in terms of simple music.

The Invention of Fiction and Lies

The earliest human stories would have related to essential survival such as food, sex and protection. With increasing brain development and comprehension, toolmaking, fire building and group hunting would lead to increased social networking, and expanding storytelling songs incorporated more memories and imagination. The awareness of past and future allowed *mental time-travel*, an escape from the present.

This long and winding road led to language and narratives. From it, fiction was born. The ability to invent or make up information brought the ability to stretch the truth. When children learn language today, they quickly find fiction, in great part because adults already use it.

Being human enlists storytelling not unlike a dream formulated from fact and fiction.

Most stories told over time are changed, modified, even fictionalized. We may even better define a feeling through fiction compared to the limitations of words, and its risk of misinterpretation. Poetic license remedies this in part by allowing us to twist the truth, or even make stories up. Regardless of whether real life seems wilder than fiction, the story still must be conveyed well. The inclusion of fiction in storytelling and music became another powerful way to expand the mind of those creating and for those hearing it, as they can further fictionalize themselves in the story.

Soon after becoming a songwriter, it appeared clever and creative to incorporate a wide variety of fictional characters in my music. While I didn't like the taste of whiskey, it was consumed by characters in some songs. And despite being happy, the saddest songs sometimes flowed out. It's just a song, right? Yet, it all came out of my mind. When asked during an interview how people could learn more about me, the response was simple — listen to my music. The persons and themes may seem rather unusual, perhaps with an uncanny twist, or not. Most appeared to be fictional characters quite unlike me. Or were they? Only afterwards, sometimes weeks, months, even years, do I ponder the fascinating and curious persona that created it. Ultimately, despite intermittent passing discomfort and dismay, I became happier with myself through increased awareness.

Over time more personalities flowed out and into my anthology. Like therapeutic sessions that uncover new memories in the subconscious mind, the interrelationships and perceptions appeared more apparent. The wide spectrum of feelings from a wild mind, ranging from refreshing and relieving to frightening, contributed to a healthier brain. It appears there are many versions of me hidden away, and, not unlike the works of painters, poets and sculptors, some are more obviously autobiographical.

'A Red Wine Cork in a White Wine Bottle'

This was the first line to the song "Red Wine Cork," which came to me after lecturing at a conference in Vail, Colorado. My talk was about the brain and how some people appear more awkward, quirky, and have an uneasy time navigating through society.

After speaking, I stopped at the hotel wine bar. While looking at the different opened bottles lined up, I noticed a red wine cork in a white wine bottle. At this moment, I saw myself as a character in my lecture. The song immediately flowed out.

Real wine corks vary in structure with the greatest variation between those of reds and whites. The natural cork for red wine is longer, sturdier, and slightly porous, enough to allow very small but beneficial amounts of oxygen into the wine to help it age and improve over a longer period. White wine is usually ready for drinking much sooner, so these corks tend to be shorter and denser. (Today, many corks contain plastic, and even screw tops.)

The idea of a red wine cork in a white wine bottle symbolizes a deviation from some expected norm. My own odd, eccentric existence was a social reality assumed but never really admitted. I would come to fully realize it many months later when accepting the song as being autobiographical, my own wild and poetic twist to the age-old adage of trying to fit a square peg into a round hole.

It was one of the very first real songs I wrote after becoming a songwriter. I knew almost nothing about being a lyricist, and even less about music. While most songs are in 2/4, 3/4 or 4/4 time, I wrote "Red Wine Cork" in a stumbling and unusual 5/4 time. For a novice folk song, it was awkward, although the famous jazz standard "Take Five" by Paul Desmond and Dave Brubeck, is a 5/4 masterpiece.

While the song just flowed out and was initially pleasing, the uneasy music and quirky lyrics were not easy to perform. Musicians I enlisted to help accompany me found it difficult, too. My neighbor Ron, a retired music professor and previously an arranger for the *Ed Sullivan Show*, tried explaining the 5/4 tempo issue, but it was beyond comprehension at that point in my music journey. (I would eventually change it to 4/4.)

One theme of my lecture that day was how everyone is a unique individual. Over the years, the fact that this song continues to touch so many people helps affirm this awareness that we are all quirky, each in our own way. This helps us be more creative and special.

"Red Wine Cork" was recorded three times before I felt it represented my original feeling of the song, only recently being released as a single. It was as if my mind needed more development to process and finish it.

Over his lifetime singer-songwriter Bob Dylan attracted as much intense attention and scrutiny about his storytelling songs as almost any artist. He has eluded most of the untold numbers of questions about the meaning of his lyrics. However, Dylan's 600-plus penned song catalog is an open book to his diverse personalities, whether portraying the real, the imagined, or some creative combination. Sam Shepard wrote, "Dylan is an invention of his own mind."

Many of us are reinventing our own minds through storytelling music. Just as storytelling can ignite the mind, and be further expanded with a strong visual component, such as a music video, the addition of movement further enlists the brain. Let's dance!

The Storytelling Dance

Do you wanna dance? It's a form of storytelling too, beyond just tapping your finger or foot to a song, it's tapping the whole body. The joy of dancing begins in the brain and flows down to the toes, helping the mind move the body for untold benefits. It's no surprise that dancing is used to prevent and help a wide range of health problems, including treatment of neurological movement disorders such as Parkinson's disease.

If you wanna dance, it's a great way to sneak more physical activity, fun and added brain benefits into your life, one song at a time!

Easy dancing is something that can be done at home for great aerobic benefits in people of all ages. It's great as your only exercise and can serve as a warmup and cooldown, or as a cross-training activity to complement other workouts. It's also a powerful tool in rehabilitation, and a wonderful developmental brain-body stimulus for children.

The secret to the joy and benefits of dancing is that it only takes a single song. And there's no need to leave home, change clothes or have a long session. Your brain and body can accumulate dance benefits over the course of a day, week or month, one song at a time. Turn on your dance mode whenever you have a moment or two. A song in the morning or during lunch, more later in the day, and suddenly you amass many benefits.

You can also plan longer sessions if you want by finding live music, taking lessons or having a party. Whether the music comes from speakers or earbuds, is live, or played all in your mind, it can work anywhere, anytime. Bop around the kitchen while cooking, twirl to your favorite tune when cleaning, sway while waiting for a bus, or gently move when singing in the shower. You can ballroom dance with a partner, tango, waltz, or rumba, or go freestyle — do what moves you and is fun.

For almost everyone, dancing is a safe, effective physical activity to help improve muscular balance, enhance cardiovascular fitness and reduce excess body fat. It's good for bones too, and dancing can increase flexibility without the need for stretching. It can improve neuroplasticity, help compensate for brain injury, disease and aging, and increase cognitive performance, including learning and memory.

If you've not been very active or danced much lately, build up slowly with very easy movements. Gradually enlist more muscles and joints throughout the body to your personal tolerance. Keep it simple and make it fun. Wear flat comfortable shoes that fit well, or go barefoot. While dancing alone works well, finding the right partner to share the enjoyment is great too.

No doubt most people have favorite dance songs. Two dance music videos of my songs include "Secret Lover" and "Do It Again." Just watching these can trigger the brain to start moving muscles. (My website also has a large playlist of dance songs.)

So put on some music, kick off your shoes, and dance your way to a better brain. Become part of the story and tell your own.

14
Sharing Song Stories

Does life imitate art or does art imitate life? As an artistic expression, songs are often stories, easily recognized as personal, individual, unique and a human form of self-psychoanalysis. Sometimes for the storyteller they are a back-and-forth internal dialogue between the conscious and subconscious mind. You play both roles: psychiatrist and patient. You're also in the audience awaiting a presentation of the next creative expression. It may come in the form of temporary answers, momentary conclusions, theories, hypotheses or otherwise our personal appearances of free associations all in neat little packages. Like all art, these manifestations are provisional. Leonardo da Vinci said that "Art is never finished, only abandoned." For this reason, the riddle of whether life imitates art or art imitates life may simply be that both are one and the same.

Most important is that in the meantime we have many of these expressions to release, share, give away and delve into. Beethoven said, "Don't only practice your art, but force your way into its secrets." As I wrote in my song "History of Secrets," they *must be freed*:

Got a history of secrets running through my life
The misty little signatures humming to my strife
The story of these secrets, windblown little seeds
The glory of the undisclosed are privileges indeed
  We always have to buy much more than we need
And keep the rest inside, please
We always have to sigh at all the things indeed
This history of secrets must be freed
This history of secrets will now be freed
  The silly little secrets the grand ones deep inside
The dark ones and those that shine it's here they all reside
This history of secrets rushing through my life
Unending dedications blushing to my strife
  We always have to buy much more than we need
And keep the rest inside, please
We always have to sigh at all the things indeed
This history of secrets must be freed
This history of secrets will be freed
This history of secrets will now be freed

When reading or listening to storytelling songs, we see or feel ourselves within them. When performing them, we share ourselves with the world, expressing ourselves with anyone who will listen. It provides a way to touch others and be touched back. The story of *Bethasia* is one example.

'Oh, Bethasia '

It was my first music gig at a bustling eclectic restaurant in a college town. A party of three waited for a table as I began my next song. This was also at that point the largest audience of my young performance career. The loud Saturday crowd was a bit overwhelming. Luckily, I thought, most people would not really hear the music well enough.

During my first set, the three waiting customers drifted past me to be seated, apparently a young student with her father and mother following in line behind her. Their table, the last open one, would be in the far corner of the restaurant. I had the idea the father would have preferred a quieter eatery, but this was where they had found themselves. They began mulling over the vegetarian menu — food that was not that great, but cheap, including a large salad bar. This inexpensive fare ensured a steady flow of young vibrant customers.

During my earlier career, observing people's actions was an important assessment practice. Profiling helped me to better understand individuals I worked with, especially athletes. This student seemed physically fit, probably a freshman in the middle of her first semester, sitting quietly sipping her lemon-spiked water. Awkwardly, she tried to converse with what seemed like two strangers — her parents — tensely talking to her. But most of the table time appeared to be quiet and uneasy. To an observer like me, the scene felt painful.

It was time to play another song.

By the first chorus, the transformation was evident. Her facial expression changed, not quite to a smile but certainly an obvious easing of tension. An upgraded sitting posture followed. The music had reached her, and she couldn't let go.

And it felt as if she touched me back. I imagined her being impelled to leap up, arms spread wide to sing out the song's mighty chorus as if performing in a rock opera or sensational choir.

It appeared, I hoped, that the music set her free . . . at least for that evening.

Having experienced similar situations in a clinical setting or an athletic field, this unfolding event felt familiar to me. However familiar, it was also my first time to have someone reflect the joy of my music back to me — like a dream never dreamt that leapt to life.

The song that so vividly affected this young student was "Oh, Bethasia." Written in Los Angeles and recorded in Nashville, the character's name is one I made up. After writing this song, it would take a couple of years for me to fully appreciate it, and how compelling the story of *Bethasia* was, especially the journey of her many musical and lyrical components.

As the party of three made their return trip through the still-crowded restaurant to the exit, single file, father first, the student ambled a bit as she walked by me. After a quick glance at her parents, she turned toward me to share her first big smile of the evening. It was much more than a thank you or even a grand applause. I nodded and smiled too as if to say, "Thank you, 'Bethasia'".

Tell Me *Your* Story

Think about how often you tell a story, real or not, merely in your own mind or out loud to others. Even if you don't have all the words, no doubt the *feelings* of a storyline are there. Even Homer and Shakespeare would have started the same way.

Like early humans, when we sing our own song or tell our story, it conveys stronger emotion compared to when telling someone else's. For many years in the music industry songwriters worked for publishers and wrote stories for others to record. But that changed. Think about some of your favorite storytelling songwriters: Joni Mitchell, Bob Dylan, Carole King, Paul Simon. This upsurge started in the 1950s and 60s, adding authenticity to performances by their own songs just like our ancestors.

Listen to a favorite strong storytelling song. If you need a recommendation, consider "Taxi" by Harry Chapin, or my song, "Alabama-Mexico." Feel the story. For a longer one, the amazing storytelling journey "Tommy" by The Who is a treasure.

Now it's your turn. Think about one of your stories — no doubt you have many hidden away. How could you reveal this personal short story? Here is a happy mind-expanding routine that can bring out more of your natural creative expressions and be fun:

- Decide which story you want to tell. Keep it short and simple for now.
- It could be as words, sketches, photos, a poem or song, or some combination.
- It need not be shared with anyone else but you unless you want.
- Take your time: a day, week or month, there's no rush, no deadline.

We all have feelings about life. For a songwriter, this means there is always a song ready to come out. Like an electrical outlet whose wires contain electrons waiting to flow out once something is plugged into it, these creations leap from our conscious and subconscious memories.

As a voracious music consumer in the 1960s, the awareness that singer-songwriters had a special human connection with listeners was clear. It was more apparent years later when working with some of them. Becoming a songwriter uncovered the other half of this two-way intense human connection.

Inspiration is a natural feature of a healthy brain. Prolific periods are based more on our environment than any need to seek inspiration. In my experience, so-called writer's block, which is too common a symptom, is an indication that something has temporarily gone astray in the brain — find it and fix it and creativity returns. Even for the beginner, start by writing anything no matter how simple, short or silly. That important foundation allows more creative self-expression.

A newly born song in its simplest, most basic form, can sound the most passionate. Singing along with just an acoustic guitar can help communicate the bare essence of the newly created feeling. This is one reason why solo singer-songwriter performances can be so powerful for listeners.

The science of storytelling is a simple art form. It is breathtaking for our brains, even more so when linked with music as it was from the beginning. We have the potential to sing and hear songs the same way as our earliest ancestors, with heartfelt emotion and sincerity that brings out our inner child and improves human performance. Storytelling music can make our minds spin, bend and expand, and go where we have never gone before — even beyond the imagination.

15

Singer-Songwriter Narratives

Music is a common thread entwining each of our lives and running throughout society as a whole. We identify with songwriters through their music and see ourselves in what they produce. Their music opens the book of their brain and that of ours as well. Singer-songwriters often hold more prominence in our society than most others, including political leaders. It's because musicians touch our hearts and souls and share a sense of closeness with us even though we do not know them personally.

Many can remember exactly where they were the day John Lennon died but they could not tell you who was president then, or what films or books were popular that year. Moreover, after the passing of a songwriter, their music sales often skyrocket and interest in their music can persist for years, as if death is the ultimate marketing tool. Research shows death-related publicity and marketing triggers considerable nostalgic reactions, especially personal feelings of consumer's own mortality. Joni Mitchell's words ring true, *we don't know what we've got till it's gone.*

As a celebration of their music, this chapter touches on some of their stories from a clinical perspective.

Johnny Cash's Brain

It was a few months after I became a songwriter that Johnny Cash asked for my help in restoring his health. Johnny still had a musical mission, but his condition had been severely failing. I traveled to his home in Hendersonville, Tennessee, and together, we devised a strategy to improve his physical and mental health. This included the use of music and biofeedback so he could write and play again.

The challenge would prove daunting. This was not because his health had been quite neglected and he was frail, nor was it due to the many years of well-publicized illegal drug and alcohol abuse — he'd not used either for many years. Rather, it was due to the *dozens* of pharmaceutical drugs prescribed by other practitioners.

While my discussions with his healthcare team early on appeared positive, especially following his rapid improvements, they were resistant to address these prescriptions, which came with drug interactions and side effects that hampered both Johnny's and my efforts. He regularly took more than 30 prescriptions, and at the time of his death that number increased to over 40. The issue of unnecessary prescriptions was not just my opinion but those of other practitioners as well.

Despite this we forged ahead. Johnny's strong will and work ethic enabled him to improve many aspects of his health and accomplish more of his goals.

When I first met Johnny, he was relegated to invalid status — in a wheelchair wearing leg braces and prescribed special shoes. After evaluating him these also appeared unnecessary, and further contributed to poor health. In addition to the obvious difficulty this posed on a man who wanted to be active, it was also embarrassing for him.

Utilizing manual biofeedback and other techniques that encouraged the brain to make better contact with weakened muscles, Johnny quickly could take a few unsteady but pain-free steps. After a couple of days, eliminating the need for braces, special shoes, and more movements out of the wheelchair, he soon was able to take upwards of 100 steps. More improvements came in the following weeks during my monthly visits. These included walking outside, riding a stationary bike, venturing into the pool and eventually walking up and down steps.

Other biofeedback approaches included certain eye-hand coordination activities that would stimulate the small muscles and nerves in the fingers of both hands, a first step to playing the guitar again. His inability to see and write would be addressed with visual rehabilitation — using a large pad and a thick black, felt-tip marker. We started with images that his brain could barely recognize, then larger letters, eventually leading to words on paper. Then one day he played and sang a new song for me.

Johnny worked hard to make significant improvements and increase his quality of life over the months. But despite reducing a few of the meds, the Medical Devil was still there. The excessive use of legal drugs remained and would become a significant problem. While away, I learned of an acute episode of severe intestinal distress, and he was hospitalized; now he was on 43 prescriptions in the name of health.

Johnny soon returned home, and I met him there. The next day we were sitting in his office planning how to regroup. He suddenly but casually turned to me and just said it was time. I was not sure what he meant until a couple of hours later when he went into respiratory distress and quickly returned to the hospital; he would pass on a few hours later.

Though ultimately Johnny's escape from the Medical Devil proved to be death itself, the lesson leaves us wondering what might have been possible had there been better overall care. Certainly, the health improvements he achieved during the final months of his life may provide an important clue to this unanswered question.

Johnny's Last Song

It was part of his therapy. Johnny's creative expressions were often associated with his love of trains and his health. His very last song portrayed taking a deep breath — perhaps a deeper allegorical tune than the song itself portrays. Originally titled *Asthma Like the 309*, the word "asthma" would be dropped from the title. It was like the first single he ever recorded, "Hey Porter," from 1955, a train song.

Flying to Nashville I felt a song coming out of my brain and wrote it on a scrap piece of paper. Realizing it was for Johnny, I couldn't wait to find time to play it for him. But when I arrived at his house, he had one too.

He played and sang what would be his first new song in some time. It was very emotional sitting in his cabin studio while the song was recorded. Sadly, it would be his last. This song still breathes deep in my soul.

I never got to play my song for him. It would eventually be recorded ("Nowhere to Run") and when performed live, I introduce it just by saying, "This one's for Johnny."

Bob Dylan

Musical freedom has been a powerful voice for centuries, with artists speaking out against many socio-economic-political ills. Singer-songwriters tell these stories in their own special ways, hoping to unite the world and go well beyond what the media or politicians are willing to do to expose certain injustices. Bob Dylan is one of the best at this.

Not only did Dylan write great songs, he won some music industry battles benefiting music listeners to this day. He refused to give in to demands that songs be only two or three minutes long for the radio, while fearlessly expressing sensitive themes that became popular despite his rough, rambling voice and relatively simple guitar playing.

Originally part of the protest movements in the early 60s, Dylan tirelessly wrote about many personal and social issues while regularly reinventing himself. He voiced this early in 1964 when singing, "Ah but I was so much older then, I'm younger than that now." His brain continued expanding over seven-plus decades. In 2016 he was awarded a Nobel Prize in Literature.

Recently, I was listening to Dylan's eight-minute, thirty-second song "Hurricane." It's the story of champion boxer Rubin Hurricane Carter, a Black man wrongly convicted of a 1966 triple murder in New Jersey. After reading Carter's newly released autobiography almost a decade following the incident, Dylan visited him in prison. Afterwards he co-wrote "Hurricane" with Jacques Levy and raised money at a Madison Square Garden concert for Carter's legal fees. It would take another decade before Hurricane was freed, with the judge stating that the prosecution's case was based on racism rather than reason, concealment rather than disclosure.

While listening to this song a parallel with a recent social trauma became evident — Covid-19. The response to the pandemic, according to some scientists, was also not reasonable with many facts concealed or unreported by the media and politicians. (Please listen or read the lyrics to fully appreciate the parallels noted here.)

The injustices of Hurricane and Covid-19 were obscured in distorted facts, emotional accusations, confusions and contradiction and devastations — with the former being a man representing the personification of prejudice, the latter a preventable global tragedy. Hurricane was yet another social wakeup call on racism; covid another healthcare calamity. As both stories unfolded, more people became upset, especially after the Hurricane story was heard and as public sentiment about the pandemic shifted.

While some songs have conveyed covid's story, none like the narratives expressed early in the pandemic:

Our leaders have taken a crisis and turned it into a tragedy; the magnitude of this failure is astonishing.

During this public crisis, political leaders have demonstrated that they are dangerously incompetent.

The truth is neither liberal nor conservative.

Dylan did not write these lyrics, although he could have. These comments about Covid-19 appeared in the medical publication *The New England Journal of Medicine* (October 2020, "Dying in a Leadership Vacuum"). This conservative, traditional journal published *lyrics* of social injustice, unprecedented in their 200-year storied history.

The Carter case, part of a long sad history of racial injustice, was made public to millions through Dylan's song; the mismanaged pandemic wrongly touched billions, virtually everyone on the planet.

The *Journal of the American Medical Association* also highlighted inequalities, including vaccine distribution and health care. It emphasized that the U.S. was among the world's poorest performers in pandemic response, along with a failing global response, undervaluing science and weak public health infrastructure.

Covid misinformation and mistrust spawned battles everywhere, not just between political factions but within families and friends, between U.S. states, within the European Union and other geopolitical units.

The three scientific covid papers I published with Professor Paul Laursen often countered the narrow media and political rhetoric in an up-front, clinical way. We echoed many other scientists, reporting on information about covid that was available but untold.

Dylan wrote that "justice is a game." In the case of covid, a microscopic virus brought its own hurricane, drawing into play the usual suspects: Politicians and corporate conglomerates wrapped in big money, with the media going along for the ride.

The pandemic's misplaced blame on a virus ignored two greater tragedies that contributed: The 40-plus-year *overfat pandemic*, a primary cause of chronic disease and infections, and the global prevalence of vitamin D-deficiency. Both were swept under the rug by the media, politics and big business. Meanwhile, the junk-food industry profited immensely from it all. Using tax dollars, the U.S. government funded vaccine development, with big pharma estimated to have raked in over $100 billion.

Covid continues impairing brain-body health including dramatic rises in suicide, domestic violence, depression and weight-gain. The global economy shrank by 4.3 percent in 2020, declining by some $10 trillion, a devastation like The Great Depression and the two world wars.

Like Hurricane Carter, hindsight seems 20/20 — he remained in prison for almost 20 years. An accurate picture of covid is slowly emerging thanks to more data and published research; however, it will be a long recovery and shameful legacy.

That's the story of Hurricane and Covid-19. But it won't be over until society clears the justice game board and makes equality a reality. Until then, we still have personal control and the ability to become our own champions of the world.

Nick Drake's Brain

We all have unique brains, making each of us who we are. We all also have injured brains, too, and adapt in some fashion for better or worse. Nick Drake's brain followed both paths. He was an English singer-songwriter whose work in the late 1960s and early 70s influenced many popular artists, including Lucinda Williams, Peter Buck of REM, The Dream Academy, Kate Bush and Aimee Mann. He remains revered by many popular singer-songwriters.

It's important to write about Nick's brain because it was the source of his songs, who he was, and how he eventually influenced millions.

Nick died in 1974 at the age of 26 from an overdose of a prescription antidepressant. He never achieved great acclaim in his lifetime, but in 1999, his song "Pink Moon" was part of the great success of an automobile TV ad. It suddenly shed light on his genius. Decades later, he has almost 2 million monthly listeners on Spotify.

Brain injuries can sometimes result in wildly ranging behaviors. This can be likened to a coin — one side is ripped with various manners of mental pain and anguish, the other side with remarkable creative expression. I won't dwell on the negative here, as I am more interested in the legacy of Nick's music and what it means for others.

A better understanding of how Nick's brain worked could help lead us to better understand and expand our minds. It also may allow us to experience his music in a brighter light. It seems Nick recognized his creative talent, and the accompanying quirkiness, eclectic self-venturing and aberrant behavior. "Helplessly strong" was how someone close described him.

Individual brains adapt to life in different ways. Some fall outside the so-called norm in doing so and may be viewed by peers as rather odd and sometimes difficult. Many clinicians see the same situation as a neurodevelopmental disorder. Some individuals who are characterized by social difficulties and inappropriate behaviors may be brain injured, such as on the autism spectrum. On one end are young people unable to cope with life requiring constant care. On the other, individuals exhibit more mild features of oddness and uncomfortable social situations.

It seems evident that Nick Drake's brain was somewhere on this spectrum.

Some on this spectrum find music is their safe place in life, albeit on their own terms. This typically involves divergent thinking and out-of-the-box creativity. Their intense imagination is innovative and inspiring, and often their lone joy. Relationships with family, friends and lovers can't keep up. Many become superstars in their fields: Amadeus Mozart appears to be another, and Albert Einstein used his musical passion to complement and even facilitate his work.

It's evident that Nick's condition was treatable, and the extreme deterioration preventable. Sadly, he did not receive the type of help he needed, even by the standards of the times.

Fortunately, Nick Drake's brain found a way — through music — to adapt to life's challenges, at least for enough time to allow some of his creativity to flow out. Acclimating to verbal and non-verbal miscommunication still enabled him to write great lyrics thanks to poetic license that gave sound to words, rather than mere figures on a page. And he compensated as best as possible to behavioral and social difficulties. This process of adaptation was the opportunity to joyfully obsess on his craft — his own music therapy.

Unfortunately, he was not able to adequately adapt, and the stressors continued to accumulate. Thus, the condition of Nick Drake's brain worsened.

It's not a stretch to claim that early exposure to music, even before birth, probably extended Nick's life. Likewise, the love his family had for him. People with brain injuries are often fraught with misdiagnoses, medication use and abuse, and psychotherapy that offers little or no success, or worse. It appeared that Nick tried to tolerate all this the best he could. I can't help but feel that he wanted his brain to heal itself since his doctors could not do so.

Early family music influences — a common ingredient in virtually all great musicians — was followed by further study in school and growing up during the mass music explosion of the times. This combination allowed Nick Drake's brain to accomplish something spectacular.

His songs were all his own, and more than special. Today they still embody a spectrum of his many personalities creatively expressed. He seemed to ride the wave of life, grasping hold for survival before eventually drowning.

Still, none of us will ever really know Nick Drake's brain, save for the music he left us. His songs are all short stories, ones he may or may not have tried to interpret but left for us to elucidate.

As Nick's brain fell further into dysfunction, he eventually became withdrawn from everyone. Near the end, it became mentally and physically difficult for him to complete a song in the studio, perhaps calling out for help he knew could not reach him. At age 26 he struggled to sing ". . . growing old and I wanna go home . . ." His downward spiral spewed various symptoms of painful vicious patterns of impaired behavior until the very end.

Thus, we are left with the relics of Nick Drake's brain, something that resides in all of us. The person and the singer-songwriter one and the same.

It's not easy delving into the brain of someone I never met, is no longer living, and who left almost no medical history. But it was clear how frighteningly similar Nick's story is with familiar cases I've witnessed during my career. Combined with public information from Nick's family, friends and colleagues, clues about his behavior and creative expressions, especially from his music, it was a process not unlike a Sherlock Holmes mystery. In addition to my healthcare experiences, as a singer-songwriter I can relate firsthand to the inner workings of the brain's personal and deepest creative expressions.

The Beatles' Brains

Imagine the sheer power of music, so dynamic that it helped launch humanity. This force of nature eventually brought us the Beatles, who in one short decade sparked a dramatic global expansion of immeasurable musical and cultural-social change. As a collective, the Fab Four revealed the universe inside their brains to billions of others, transcending generations and continuing their influence today.

With their first album, supported by fifth-brain producer George Martin, they were a single bolt of musical lightning pushing the limits of perfection, trusting no boundaries or restrictions, with their musical minds running 24/7. Yet the few short years of touring, mania and massive success also generated huge stress, expressed simply as *Help!*

By the mid-60s, after about 2,900 intense global performances, weary and less fun, the Beatles ceased touring. Their personal musical evolutions continued maturing. Psychedelics and meditation further expanded their minds, and family life brought new priorities. The door opened to a transition through twin albums, *Rubber Soul* and *Revolver*.

The intense, innovative music continued at astounding paces. Adapting to their status required regular rebalancing of their individualities, families, the band, and a growing overbearing business stress — expressed in songs through *Abby Road* and *Let It Be*.

And in the end, the Beatles bowed out, breaking up on the highest note. We didn't want the Beatles to end. Was it better to burn out or to fade away?

The Beatles did neither. Despite the media hype, the clinical evidence indicates they had to disband to avoid burnout. And, since their individual creative passions were still rapidly expanding, fading away was not an option. Instead, it was the perfect adaptation.

It's not better to burn out — the physical and mental-emotional collapse of human performance. Nor to fade away with an injured brain, or worse. But there are more than these two lose-lose options. A third is adaptation through our natural survival process of recovery involving the previously discussed HPA axis. This adeptness, the great escape, can forge new roads to expand creative journeys. This healthy but difficult transition was the final great feat of the Beatles, allowing each an entrance to a brave new world.

Throughout society burnout is a rite of passage, and too many let themselves go too far. Younger creative, passionate geniuses often rock around the clock, driving themselves for more creative expressions. Those who strive to outdo themselves and their peers are most vulnerable to mental fatigue and burnout. As exemplified in business, evidence of burnout over age 50 is 59 percent, age 35-50, 84 percent, and those 18-34, 94 percent. Burnout is preventable and treatable, whether we're discussing an individual or a group of four rapidly expanding creative brains.

Today, the work of the Beatles' brains still influences and inspires music, culture and society, including the clinical and scientific community.

George Harrison's Clinical Case

While each of the Beatles has a fascinating story, George Harrison is associated with a uniquely interesting one.

The deep expressions behind this quiet Beatle's mind reveals much about his secret personalities and our own brains. While Harrison's vocal sounds were not as loud in most Beatles marvelously mixed songs, among my earliest musical exercises to improve brain function was mentally pulling out these hidden gems. Then I'd do this same by finding all his guitar parts. Consciously hearing the depth of the songs produced greater joy. In photos and videos, one could virtually see his body language, postural reflections of the brain's strain to reach deep inside to direct those feelings.

Harrison's expressions are a special feature, sometimes escaping the restrictions of Western music. And, creating dissonant chords to express the stress of touring was another example: an E7 chord with an F on top, which triggered other musicians, including John Lennon, to follow suit.

In addition to Harrison's music draped inside our minds, came an increased understanding of the brain itself. It came in the form of *cryptomnesia*, a state previously known but understood by few.

Normally, the sensory input of music is retained as conscious and subconscious memories, influencing our feelings. During creative output, while translating our feelings, potentially any memory could appear. We rely on our brains to build a better song — one that's unique from all others, including our previous creations.

Among the great Harrison songs is "My Sweet Lord." But some of this song's music unknowingly sounded like another musician's tune, one he may have heard years earlier in the throes of Beatlemania. In what became a long legal case, the lawyers called foul, and Harrison was accused of copying music from "He's So Fine" written by Ronnie Mack and recorded by the Chiffons. In the court's decision, which set precedent for many later copyright cases, it was made clear that Harrison did not plagiarize on purpose, but rather it was a subconscious event enlisting old memories. Nonetheless, Harrison was fined. More people became aware of this fascinating mind game that virtually everyone plays in their own brains.

Cryptomnesia is a state of unknowingly, subconsciously using a past memory and thinking it's uniquely our own. In short, it's a fascinating brain fart. Having spent much of my clinical career helping people improve brain performance, the Harrison case remains intriguing. When becoming a songwriter, the phenomenon became more fascinating as I would sometimes inadvertently do the same thing with my music. All human brains are influenced by other brains in all fields of endeavor, a trend not unusual.

What's your storytelling song? An earlier chapter discussed writing your story. Now you can put it to music if that's not already been done.

16

The Music of Exercise and Sports

In the book *Musicophilia,* Oliver Sacks explores the profound relationship between music and the mind. The famed neurologist suffered a serious leg injury while mountain climbing, and described how he was able to get down the mountain before dark by singing "The Old Volga Boatman." He "musicked" along to rhythms and melodies that made his mind overcome the pain. Later, in the hospital, he repeatedly listened to a Mendelssohn violin concerto. After weeks of struggling to walk, he found that "the concerto started to play itself with intense vividness in my mind. In this moment, the natural rhythm and melody of walking came back to me . . . and along with this the feeling of my leg as alive, as part of me once again."

While music's motivation for the brain is undeniable, it includes the physical response to it promoting another form of natural power — body movement. Both create a beautiful blend of art and science. As one, music and motion are greater than the sum of the parts. It's virtually impossible to not move to music, which would also not exist without the physical motor skills to create sound.

Encompassing one common human expression, music and movement create a global language, fundamental to our social and cultural roots. We usually experience and witness this during international sports events. This shared coexistence is a natural promotion of peace that transcends differences in racial and ethnic, political, religious and other avenues. We see it in children who are known to promote prosocial behavior when exposed to music. Whether a single individual action or one that influences our world, that most important first step begins in our musical brain.

Music can also prepare us for physical actions from helping us get fit to reaching goals like running a 26-mile marathon, and others between and beyond. And it can complement various types of mental or physical therapies including rehabilitation.

The use of music can be individual. Consider that those with certain personality traits prefer background music while working, driving or performing other tasks. For others, silence is best. Yet silence enlists imagining music, even if subconscious.

A pro baseball player plugs in earbuds to hear favorite tunes while putting on a game face. Soon, a special personal song accompanies his name as both are blared out over the stadium's speakers. But like all others on the field, by the time they are ready to hit, throw the ball or run the bases, the outside music is stopped. The mind even mutes the crowd noise. This is the brain on autopilot.

The DMN

The *default mode network* or DMN is autopilot. A connection of numerous brain areas that internally processes many external events at one time. It's multitasking at its best, allowing optimal physical performance of familiar activities, enlisting memories of previously learned skills and subconsciously planning for upcoming actions. Most experienced race-car drivers go into it, as do tennis players, golfers and other athletes. Likewise, performing musicians. We all use it, including during everyday driving.

The DMN also is critical to our effective use of imagination and creativity, and night- and day-dreaming. It also enlists alpha.

However, the DMN can be quickly deactivated, diminishing performance when we shift the brain into a state of *intentional focus*. This puts us into beta, and why texting while driving is dangerous. Music can interfere the same way, and why our baseball player performs best without it. Some sports organizations ban personal music during competition, and some states have rules about driver's use of headphones and earbuds, and even devices themselves — Oregon has a "no touch" law for phones in the vehicle.

Autopilot can be impaired when in a high beta state, including excess talking just like internal chatter interferes with meditation. In addition, neuroticism and other brain injuries, physical trauma, especially to the head and neck, chronic pain, and dementia can reduce autopilot. As with driving and competitive sports, an impaired or turned off DMN can interfere with exercise, too.

When first learning the details of an activity like tennis or guitar, we rely on intentional focus. Eventually, as we no longer must think of each of the many details, the DMN takes over, and we play on autopilot, using a massive amount of subconscious processing to automatically perform well. While the brain normally uses a significant amount of energy for healthy function, 90 percent of it goes to an active DMN.

Our past music experiences that lead to better brain function bring the important question of whether listening *during* exercise, playing sports, or competing is useful or not. The DMN is so valuable during exercise but may not be as effective during music listening. Instead, turn the music off and listen to your body, allowing the DMN to promote smoother, more accurate and efficient movements requiring less effort and energy. In other words, let the brain conduct the body.

The DMN is described as a meditative state like healthy daydreaming (using imagination), mental time travel (thinking about past and future), and an almost effortless undistracted *unaware awareness*. It appears to encourage both introspection and mind wandering which also enlists imagination. (Some types of meditation encourage mind wandering while others aim to reduce it.)

Beethoven was deaf for years, only *hearing* music with his imagination. These musical hallucinations are common in acquired deafness.

During REM sleep the DMN is also very active. Scientists think this enables dreams to rehearse or simulate potential future events to prepare for them. In addition, this DMN-REM activity helps consolidate memories, both in preparation of and after new learning, another reason why sleep quality and quantity are vital for a great brain. Physical activity can also be impaired in those with sleep disorders due to aging-like deterioration in muscles.

The dopamine system drives the brain's feeling of reward, also controlling movement and coordination using the DMN. Dopamine is activated by music listening, imagining, playing — and in the anticipation or prediction of them. The passionate quartet of dopamine, the DMN, physical activity and music existed in the earliest humans.

Other benefits of the DMN may include:

- Protecting the brain and promoting healthy aging.

- Its accompanying alpha state.

- Encouraging neuroplasticity.

- Allowing continued improvements in the activities being performed.

- Preventing depression, anxiety, attention deficit, post-traumatic stress disorders, memory loss and cognitive decline.

Listen to Your Body

When learning details of a specific physical activity, intentional focus is required, and music listening can interfere. When performing physical activities already learned, hearing music may not be best either. Instead, let the brain listen to the body. It's a powerful meditation the DMN regulates. Every step we take, each move we make, sends billions of messages to the brain where they are quickly analyzed so others can be sent back to the body for appropriate ongoing adjustments in movement. External music can compete with and distract from these many sensations.

Free feeling in motion is one of the wonderful features of physical activity and sport. It's a meditation that goes beyond just sensing the muscles that move the arms and legs. The heart beats (another muscle), the breath moves in and out (the diaphragm and abdominal muscles), and our joints, ligaments, tendons, and other structures send and receive vital bits of information to and from the brain. Fortunately, autopilot manages the process. If you've never meditated on motion, it makes for an amazing aspect of working out.

Likewise, for our external environment. Merging with nature, whether a city park or far-off trail, is full of its own beautiful sensory sounds, smells and sights. The woods and fields, the grassy flowered knolls, and trees induce another brain rejuvenation. This practice of Japanese *shinrin-yoku* or *forest bathing* can powerfully reduce stress. The value of a single workout, or just being there, is potent enough to last days. Music listening during this activity can interfere.

Listening for the Wrong Reasons

While marketing encourages the use of music during exercise, research shows that listening to appropriately selected songs exert a range of work-enhancing (ergogenic) and psychological effects on the body. The process underlying this auditory–motor coupling is called entrainment. Reported short-term effects include increased exercise intensity, distraction from fatigue and pain, improving arousal, mood and motivation, and inducing a sense of power.

While some researchers have hailed these effects, likening them to illegal performance-enhancing drugs, especially when using loud driving rhythmic music, some clinicians are aware of potential long-term harms. Research shows that these ergogenic effects can eventually lead to reductions in health and performance.

Music can mesmerize people who may not realize the potential hidden harm. This musical mentality can drive the popular myth of *no-pain no-gain*, inducing physical, biochemical and mental-emotional stress. In short, it can create a condition of fit but unhealthy people, including athletes at all levels.

The fallout is remarkably common. Pushing fitness at the expense of health can lead to physical injuries like a pulled hamstring or knee pain, even career-ending impairments in competitors. Many retired athletes have life-long disabilities. Overtraining can reduce immune function, leading to increased infections and illness, and depression, anxiety, and more serious mental impairment, diminishing performance along the way. The metabolic effects are staggering too — more than ever those who exercise have rising rates of excess body fat. These are well-recognized components of the *overtraining syndrome*, a stress pattern also called *burnout* in executives, parents, teachers, students and others.

Hollywood promotes the same intense driving music that can overstimulate the brain. Songs from movies like *Rocky* and *Chariots of Fire* glorify no pain no gain. Just watching a movie relaxing on the couch can rouse the nervous system and raise the heat rate.

Some have become strongly dependent on music's emotional trigger to power a workout. Loud driving rhythms run through earbuds, gyms and training centers hoping it distracts from pain and fatigue, elevates mood, and drives longer training at faster paces, not unlike caffeine.

While music can't completely cover the pain and fatigue during exercise, it can make the activity feel more positive, even enjoyable. This misguided motivation distorts messages to the brain. Pain is a warning that something is not right, like an impending injury. Fatigue reflects the onset of muscle weakness, reduced performance, and is a precursor to further injury. (During competition athletes don't cover pain and fatigue but contain it, so it doesn't distract as much from performance.)

In addition to interfering with the DMN and reducing performance, other potential problems associated with music listening during physical activity include:

- Risk of hearing damage with commonly used high volumes.
- Raising intensity and heart rate beyond one's planned goal or ability, risking overtraining, and shifting metabolism to burn less stored fat for energy.
- The risk of accidents, especially in the presence of people, animals, equipment, motorized vehicles and uneven terrain.

Those more extroverted use less of their DMN, often playing music while working and driving. In certain situations, this can be distracting for the brain. Studies show that higher involvement in auto crashes is positively associated with being extroverted. In my clinical experience working with athletes, those who listened to music during workouts were more often injured, although this needs further scientific scrutiny. In a study on snowboarding, music listening resulted in fewer injuries but increased the risk of more serious injuries requiring a visit to the emergency department.

There are two interesting exceptions to this discussion. Like the baseball player, most exercises and sports have variations in body movements based on the situation, terrain and numerous other factors. In these cases, music can be distracting and interfere with effective physical performance. For obvious reasons, this is not so in well-trained musicians:

- Experienced dancers, figure skaters, and others can successfully incorporate the DMN using musical rhythms as an expressive meditation, often not hearing other aspects of a song.

- Skilled musicians, including vocalists, engage autopilot while performing.

In these individuals, the brain's natural management of the DMN is associated with and encourages higher levels of proficiency.

The remedy

The best remedy is utilizing the beneficial components of music listening at specific times around exercise:

- Pre-exercise music can powerfully influence the workout in healthy ways, like our baseball player.

- These effects are maintained as you start working out, when silence is best.

- Post-exercise initiates recovery (when more benefits are realized than the workout itself). Music here, especially easy listening, can be very helpful.

Despite this, some people still will listen to music during exercise. If you must, here are ways to reduce the risks:

- Employ heart-rate training (exercise biofeedback) to lessen the risk of overtraining when music may take charge of the workout instead of the brain.
- Research shows slower-tempo music can also improve physical performance. It may also lower the heart rate, reduce stress and encourage autopilot mode.
- Even sedative music can improve performance.
- Avoid playing music loudly. It could make the right music wrong.

In addition, matching music to your workout can be very helpful. Just as certain songs may be best for planned easy aerobic or higher-intensity training, alternate music for specific sections of a workout can help too. For example, while warming up and cooling down avoid listening to Nirvana's "Aneurysm" and instead relax with James Taylor's "Sweet Baby James" or even Beethoven's "Moonlight Sonata."

The Warmup

Whether an easy walk or high-intensity training, actively warming up the body first is an essential feature. This applies to all exercise and sports activities including strength training, tennis, golf and others. A walking warmup is ideal. Properly done, this easy 15-minute prepping the body improves muscle circulation for more efficient movement, raises oxygen and fat-burning for energy, and increases flexibility (without the need to stretch) in the joints, ligaments, and tendons, for optimal gait and injury prevention. Throughout the warmup, gradually increase the pace while keeping it relatively easy.

Since warming up involves easy activity, easy listening music is best. Simple classical pieces, folk, soft jazz, easy country, and other relaxing songs work best.

The Middle

The warmup ends with the middle part of the workout, which varies in length depending on the total time planned. Whether easy aerobic training or high intensity, you're moving faster, so listening to faster, but not louder, music may be best. For easy aerobic training, music with a moderate beat is great, but be cautious with higher intensity faster music which could encourage overtraining.

The Cooldown

Fifteen minutes before finishing the workout, begin cooling down. Just as important as warming up, this final phase marks the key start of recovery. Regarding pace, the cooldown is merely the opposite of the warmup — a slowly descending heart rate and intensity ending with a walk. The best music is like that of the slower tempo warmup tunes.

For those just starting or resuming exercise, a shorter warmup and cooldown can be the whole workout.

Exercise Playlists

Many musical pieces fit exceptionally well with and around exercise. There are two playlists of my songs, one for easy aerobic workouts, and another for higher intensity training. They can be found with the dancing playlist: maffetonemusic.com/exercise-dance-songs

Physical activity is the essential companion to music — we're born for both. In the next chapter, this beautiful balance is blended into a *meditative dance* that can further expand the mind even beyond the previously discussed Five-Minute Power Break.

17

The Meditative Dance

In addition to its integral link to movement, especially dance, and in promoting health, music can also contribute to fitness. It enhances overall physical and mental human performance to further help reach your personal goals. While also strongly linked, health and fitness are defined differently.

While this book focuses on using music to improve health, it incorporates fitness too. I consider both as separate components of our whole being:

- Health is a balance of all bodily systems — nervous, hormonal, intestinal, immune, muscular, skeletal, etc. We can continue striving for better health.

- Fitness is the ability to perform physical movements, ranging from daily activities and easy exercise to sports and competition. Those who are physically active are more fit than those who are not. On a given day, the marathon winner is more fit than all other race competitors.

The brain-body naturally strives for a balance of health and fitness, unless we interfere through unhealthy habits like overtraining, inactivity or poor eating. Injury, illness, fatigue, pain, and other signs and symptoms indicate imbalance.

Health is obviously important, and without it building fitness is challenging. Fitness can contribute to health. Unfortunately, many people create an imbalance leading to being fit but unhealthy. Music can help improve both.

Humans are born athletes. Yet our society emphasizes no pain no gain, contributing to impaired health in some while discouraging others from exercise. Even the physical activities we perform all day, around the house or office, contribute to fitness. Developing more is simple. Comfortable short activities like easy walking can significantly improve fitness as well as measurable healthy brain aging. This workout should feel so easy that when completed one should be energized and, while unnecessary, capable of repeating it right away.

The balance of music and movement is natural meditation. It's all intricately linked not only through exercise but while enlisting very easy activities like simple finger or foot tapping, and using more muscles to clap, stamp, and sing the body's sounds. Even a bit of easy head bobbing if not extreme can powerfully enhance this bidirectional process. In short, the brain expresses itself by playing the body as its musical instrument. This meditative dance can serve as a natural shortcut to better physical and mental-emotional health and fitness.

The Five-Minute Meditative Dance

The many benefits of combining music listening, contemplation, deep breathing exercises, and the alpha state was emphasized earlier when discussing the Five-Minute Power Break. Turning this powerful activity into a unique *dance* further enhances brain-body health and fitness.

This advanced music biofeedback method is called the *Five-Minute Meditative Dance*. It integrates different physical and mental training routines into one, further encouraging enticement of the brain's DMN. For me, it's better than a runner's high.

Can we really dance while lying down? Of course. Many people already tap their way through a song not only with a finger, but move many muscles from head to toe sometimes so slightly they don't realize it.

While the previously described Five-Minute Power Break has various moving parts, the Meditative Dance enlists more muscles and coordinated activities. When first learning the details, it may best be performed:

- In silence, as external music may distract you from the necessary intentional focus.
- Incorporating easy, simple movements using minimal amounts of muscle contraction to move the toes, feet and other body parts.
- After revisiting the *marching* routine (Chapter 10) to ensure better rhythmicity.

While the value begins right away, adequate practice leads to the use of autopilot, which brings even more benefits. This mind-expanding routine can promote:

- Neuroplasticity.
- Improved cognition.
- Hormone and immune balance.
- Muscle coordination.
- Increased energy levels.
- Cardiovascular activity.
- Successful aging.

A similar more traditional dance of our physical and mental components was no doubt used by our ancestors and performed throughout history and modified across many cultures. These routines are guided by rhythm-inducing trance-like states of consciousness, like healthy hypnosis, flow states or disassociation. Commonly used routines range from religious and spiritual practices to ballet and break-dancing, like participating in exercise and competitive sports. Researchers are now mapping the mind to demonstrate the great brain-body benefits of such activities. A goal of the Meditative Dance is to create a very similar condition over a short timeframe that can be performed regularly at home or anywhere you're comfortable.

Since this is an extension of the Five-Minute Power Break, let's quickly review those guidelines:

1. Sit, recline, or lie down and relax.

2. Keep eyes closed and relaxed.
3. Position your hands or crossed arms at rest on your upper abdomen.
4. Using your diaphragm and abdominal muscles, breathe slowly, easily and deeply:
    - Inhale for about 5-10 seconds (about 75 percent of your maximum lung volume). This involves the easy pushing out and relaxing of the belly. During the last 1-2 seconds of inhalation, add slight chest expansion — enough to feel contraction of the muscles in the upper chest, and front of shoulders. (If you feel the need to yawn, just let it happen.)
    - Exhale about 5-10 seconds. This involves gently contracting the abdominal muscles (pulling them inward towards the lower spine). During the last 1-2 seconds, add a mild contraction of the pelvic floor muscles.
5. Listen to enjoyable inspiring music for about five minutes (headphones or earbuds are best).

Now you can start the Meditative Dance, using the above as a guide. Still reclining, picture your brain conducting the body's orchestra, each part a different instrument flowing with the music. This involves moving many parts, multi-tasking. Drummers do it, using hands and feet differently to continually create various musical sounds. Dancers also have wide varieties of specific physical movement routines.

Begin by gently moving the toes, tapping the fronts of your feet. As powerful structural body movements, the nerves in the toes and feet feed back to the brain in significant stimulating ways (think of getting a foot rub). While most people can tap a finger to a favorite tune, now you want to do it with your feet. But keep it simple and easy at first.

It's not necessary for wide ranges of motion as even slight movements of muscles in the fingers, hands, feet and other parts are very potent.

If your marching routine discussed earlier was successful, like the Five-Minute Power Break, you should have little or no trouble using both feet to tap alternate musical beats, like drumming.

For many, this routine may initially be easier said than done. There is a lot going on and much to learn. So you may not be relaxed yet as you focus on how to move the many muscles and body parts. As the orchestra plays, different instruments take turns while others momentarily rest. The result is the Meditative Dance.

While all this is less easy to explain, doing these combined natural activities, just like learning any physical activity, gets better over time. For some, it could take days, weeks, or longer, to get into the flow, to turn on the DMN, while others, especially dancers and drummers, usually, although not always, perform it well sooner.

Musical Suggestions

The kinds of music you use could make it easier to start. Feel free to just choose some of your favorite tunes. Those with significant rhythm will help — let drums and bass guide your movements. For example, the sounds of Santana or Buddy Holly are simple and powerful usually with a consistent tempo. Certain Beatles songs, like some classical music, have meter (time) changes within the song and may be tricky at first — ultimately not a problem as you just modify the movements like dancing.

Right now, my favorite song for this meditation is Lisa Hannigan's "Home." It's 4:59 with many soothing moving parts to put us deep into alpha while the vocals help pace our breathing. For classical, consider something like Steve Reich's "Duet" for two violins and orchestra (5:15), or the bigger "Somebody to Love" (4:57) from Queen.

Realize that there are many song-beats in between the more obvious ones you initially tap with on your finger or foot. The action of a finger tap is one; raising up preparing to tap again is another. When listening to music with a rhythm section, hear the various drum sounds and drum rolls (a series of rapidly played beats), and the bass guitar.

By now you may be dancing, while reclining or lying down, enlisting all the deep breathing muscles from the top to bottom of the torso (roof to the basement) — neck to pelvic floor — along with fingers, hands, feet and, eventually, going into autopilot will enlist other muscles to come on board like when dancing on your feet. In time you may even have an out-of-body experience.

Benefits from the Meditative Dance can begin with your first session, even if it feels difficult. As you learn the process the brain will shift from intentional focusing on the details to autopilot. Performing it at least daily can help speed the process. While it could take time to become very proficient, you are still reaping the value of a powerful brain-body dance in only five minutes.

The Five-Minute Meditative Dance can help all your other physical activities whether walking, running, cycling or swimming, even tennis, golf and other sports. It not only offers improvements in coordination of rhythm but can also impact positively on aging.

Whether you participate in competitive sports or are starting to be more active, the ability to move the body in smooth harmonic motions is a key feature of human performance.

18
Sex, Drugs, Rock 'n' Roll . . . and Food

Foods and drugs can influence our health and passions in astonishing ways. This includes how we hear, respond to, play, and otherwise relate to and remember music, even influencing whether we obtain benefits from it. Along with sex, these life's pleasures are influenced by the neurotransmitter dopamine, which joins rewarding feelings with euphoria, rendering some addicting. Truly, the brain feeds itself.

Dopamine sparks happy highs that we associate with our favorite times. It's human to remember great oldies with the accompanying shot of pleasure. Just the anticipation of gratification, including imagining a song, can elevate dopamine. So can alpha-wave states.

Dopamine also works with endorphins, endocannabinoids and oxytocin, stimulated by other feel-good experiences, such as exercise, an exciting movie or book, and time with loved ones. Pleasure is an important part of life and healthy aging.

Factors that impair dopamine include physical inactivity, hormone imbalance, poor metabolism and unnecessary meds, as well as overusing electronic devices, social media and video games. This can result in mental and physical fatigue, reduced passion and motivation, poor sleep, addictions, memory loss, depression and pain.

This chapter discusses the role of music in sex, as well as commonly used substances that strongly affect the brain, including psychedelics and cannabis, certain foods, prescription drugs, caffeine and alcohol.

Music and Sex

The modern image of rock stars is that they are having the most and best sex on the planet. The fact is, as humans, we are all rock stars.

Sexual health and fitness are states of physical, emotional and social happiness. The World Health Organization emphasizes that improving sexual wellbeing remains a public health priority across the globe.

Music and sex are linked as powerful natural creative expressions passed down from our ancestors. As a global feel-good feature of being human, they are part of our individuality. Today they are also woven into our social-cultural existence and all its many components (moral, legal, religious, behavioral, etc.). Moreover, music and sex are entwined with drugs and foods as discussed here.

Certainly, listening to oldies can bring us back in time when our maturing hormones and search for love was very human. Music's hard-wired mating calls can still be enjoyed whether we're looking for a new mate or not. We're all human, and when healthier, hormones that have great brain-body benefits also are associated with sex.

The essence is simple. Beginning in the brain, music can improve physical, biochemical and mental-emotional health and fitness. It instigates a neurohormonal cascade, triggering the hypothalamic-pituitary-adrenal axis, influencing all other glands as well. The result is a reduction of stress hormones and increases in the estrogens, testosterone and other sex hormones in men and women, further enhancing the brain for music acuity. Much of this was discussed directly or indirectly in previous chapters.

The outcome is also simple — better performance — improving wide-ranging brain-body function compatible with our individual needs.

Psychedelics

The scientific research and therapeutic use of psychedelics, a word referring to consciousness (from the Greek *mind* or *psyche*), in humans began in the 1950s. After a 40-year pause following its prohibition, renewed interest began about 20 years ago. Psychedelics have entered the scientific mainstream with clinical use in people with depression, chronic pain, alcohol, tobacco, and other addictions, stress disorders, obsessive-compulsive disorder, anorexia, end of life care and others, including brain injuries.

Music accompanying psychedelic therapy further modulates emotions, mental imagery, personal meaningfulness, and can contribute to mystical experiences.

Research shows psychedelics can enlist many brain areas to liberate creative thinking by linking our outer and inner worlds — the conscious and subconscious mind. Moreover, brain benefits can occur with a single dose and be maintained for months or years. These include positive brain rewiring, referring to neurons making new connections to boost awareness, and increasing plasticity for repair, creating a better brain. While these benefits are like those of music, it's no surprise that combining music with psychedelics is common both recreationally and clinically.

Some psychedelics (also called hallucinogens) commonly used today include:

- Psilocybin mushrooms.

- Peyote cactus (mescaline).

- LSD (lysergic acid diethylamide) synthesized from rye fungus.

- DMT (dimethyltryptamine) from Amazon jungle plants, as well as synthesized. (DMT is also naturally produced in our brain's pineal gland. Its physiologic function remains unknown, although it appears to protect the brain in part due to its anti-inflammatory actions.)

A psychoactive ingredient of cannabis is THC (tetrahydrocannabinol), having similar effects as psychedelics in a dose-dependent manner (i.e., a lower dose of psilocybin and higher THC can produce a similar experience). Research on cannabis, or marijuana, is extensive too, with similar benefits ranging from positive effects on pain, anxiety, sleep disorders and PTSD, to intestinal disease, epilepsy, glaucoma, nausea and vomiting. As such, cannabis (THC) is included in this discussion on psychedelics.

In addition to obtaining cannabis from reliable sources, the healthiest way to use it is ingestion rather than smoking. Cannabis also contains CBD (cannabidiol), which is not psychoactive, is very heat-sensitive, and has been used in patients with epilepsy, addiction, sleep disorders and problems associated with behavior and memory.

Ancestral High

Scientists say that psilocybin mushrooms were among the psychedelics ingested by our earliest ancestors. This could have further encouraged brain development, including the dopamine system. Today, all our brains and bodies have receptors for psychedelic substances. (Receptors are like doorways enabling the active chemicals to affect the brain.)

In ancient times, psychedelic use would have enhanced the senses, increasing the benefits of music, while also boosting visual effects, insightfulness, meaningfulness, social interactions and mystical experiences. For thousands of years, history describes additional therapeutic effects like cannabis use in Indian ayurvedic medicine to reduce pain, nausea, anxiety, improve appetite and sleep, relax muscles and produce euphoria.

Psychedelics are neither neurotoxic nor physically addictive, and affect the brain in fascinating ways. Normally, all sensory information entering our conscious mind from the outside world, and internally through memories and the subconscious, is first filtered by the thalamus. This prevents much of that information from reaching our conscious awareness. Psychedelics reduce this inhibition which, scientists say, can offer new insights and perspectives, especially from the subconscious where information is unprocessed, uncensored and unconstrained. This can amplify our ability to see, feel, touch, hear, think, smell and sense more of our world. Psychedelics can also promote hallucinations — seeing or hearing things that are enhanced, changed, amplified or that do not exist. (Visual hallucinations can occur normally in some individuals, called *phantom vision*, especially in those with poorer visual acuity.)

Whether using psychedelics or not, the ability to sense and process surroundings and emotions is a unique feature of highly artistic and scientifically creative people. The potential for positive influence on personality, especially openness, enhanced cognition, abstract and imaginative thinking, problem solving and intellectual engagement has led many to promote psychedelics to enrich social connectedness.

Dosing of psychedelics is important and can vary:

- Many benefits come from low to moderate doses that promote increased cognitive functions, visual skills, nontraditional thinking, increased imagination, hallucinations and access to the subconscious.

- Higher doses promote similar effects and may be more conducive to generating deep existential insights like intense meditation.

- Using about one-tenth the moderate- to high-dose, called *microdosing*, has recently become popular. Without a noticeable high, some research shows similar therapeutic effects.

In addition to clinical guided therapy, psychedelics such as psilocybin are suddenly growing in popularity again. A 2021 U.S. National Institutes of Health survey showed over seven million people aged 12 or older reported using hallucinatory psychedelics, with nearly 10 percent of U.S. adults having used psilocybin at some point in their lifetime. Separately, cannabis use is much higher having long been legal for recreational and medical use in many parts of the world. Australia has become the first country to officially recognize psychedelics as medicines.

During Covid-19, rates of reported depression by U.S. adults rose from a pre-pandemic level of 8.5 percent to 27.8 percent. Other research showed that those using psychedelics during this period reported less stress and more social support.

The guided use of psychedelics, including dosing considerations, can help reduce the risk of unpleasantness. "Bad trips" can occur if individuals are unfamiliar or uncomfortable with intense feelings and sensations, have unpleasant hallucinations or disordered thinking. Music can be helpful in these situations as well.

Brain Injury

The therapeutic use of psychedelics to support recovery from brain injury is a rapidly expanding area of clinical science. Like music, it's now being applied to various types of brain injuries like those with biochemical and mental-emotional impairments causing depression, anxiety and others noted, including PTSD. Likewise for traumatic brain injury, and those caused by stroke and neurological diseases. The clinical and scientific reasons for the success of psychedelics appear to be their influence on:

- **Neuroinflammation.** Commonly associated with and a complication of brain injuries. While most anti-inflammatory drugs may provide potential benefits, they come with the risk of significant side effects.

- **Neurogenesis.** Growing new brain cells following injury has been demonstrated using psychedelics in animals, and published research in human brains may be coming soon.

- **Neuroplasticity.** While psychedelics can promote both structural and functional neuroplasticity in so-called *normal* people without serious brain injuries, this may also become an important research focus in patients since plasticity is key to recovery.

Researchers now suggest that psychedelic-induced increases in brain complexity may help restore or improve awareness in patients with *disorders of consciousness* (DOC), a common feature of serious brain injury. While traditionally defined as minimally conscious such as a vegetative state, some define DOC more broadly as any change from complete self-awareness and arousal — not unlike other spectrum conditions. This includes those with mild brain injuries who are unable to enter an alpha state due to even minor physical, biochemical or mental-emotional traumas. This common condition contributes to a world of increasing brain injury.

The dramatic increase in psychedelic research is not surprising. Along with natural inquiry, studies from the 1950s and 60s, and millennia of historical use in mind expansion, another reason may be that before becoming professionals, many of us experienced the benefits of psychedelics.

In my mid-teens, a first psychedelic experience prompted immediate dramatic positive brain changes, breaking my illusory self like the story of Tommy in The Who's rock opera. It was my lifesaving moment. Complemented by music, it plucked me out of a lifeless existence, suddenly expanding the awareness of the world — and a universe that could be me. I began blazing my path as a new person on an amazing journey.

The experience released me. I could confront myself, battle my demons and be in the moment. My world was no longer black and white but a rainbow. It enabled adaptation from significant brain impairment that today would have various labels. While psychedelics are known to improve personality and wellbeing, this overnight revolution also expanded my perspectives, giving me a craving for learning and intellect, even physical abilities never experienced. Music felt as if I were hearing it for the first time, and my ability to easily change states of consciousness was evident. As the individual person of my existence emerged, I felt healed.

The modern field of psychedelic science is undergoing its own revolution. In an editorial in the prestigious journal *Frontiers in Neuroscience*, researchers Candance Lewis and colleagues state, "This field inspires a more complete understanding of the human condition — harkening back to days of holistic science."

Whether using psychedelics or letting nature supply the high, for music and the brain to work best we need to feed our head with nutrients from healthy foods.

Foods

What we eat strongly influences mind-expansion, music benefits, personality and especially aging. Some foods and drugs have effects that are remarkably similar, including those associated with pleasure or pain, euphoria or gloom, energy or exhaustion.

The bottom line: obtain the necessary nutrients from healthy items while avoiding junk food. This can increase mental and physical energy, promote neuroplasticity, improve sleep, reduce pain and inflammation for repair and prevention, and much more.

Junk foods have been heavily marketed as good for so long most people assume they are safe, or even healthy, and consume them. The opposing scientific and clinical consensus is often ignored. A recent *Lancet* study exemplifies how bad food contributes to more deaths than tobacco, all drugs and high blood pressure.

While marketing, media and governments make it seem complicated and confusing, it's not. Two foods most important to consider for healthy brains are carbohydrates and fats.

Carbohydrates

Junk food is the world's most common cuisine, with refined or processed carbohydrates, including sugar, the primary ingredient. Even carbs without added sugars quickly convert to sugar after consumption. About half of all carbs consumed convert to stored fat.

Eating sugar and other refined carbs can quickly and powerfully hurt the brain. After a short-term jolt from a dopamine high, even moderate amounts can impair energy, induce sleepiness, and reduce focus much like a sedative sometimes called *brain fog*. This can increase hunger and cravings for more carbs, and, despite poor energy, impair nighttime sleep. A vicious cycle can develop leading to sugar addiction.

These side effects are associated with excess insulin release — impairing metabolism toward short-term glucose energy and away from fat-burning for endurance. Eventually a serious condition called *carbohydrate intolerance* (*insulin resistance*) develops, indicated by excess body fat, especially in the belly. Even the ability to burn fat calories through exercise is compromised.

Sugar and other refined carbs are a primary cause of the global overfat pandemic. In the U.S., over 90 percent of adults and 70 percent of children have excess body fat that impairs health. This is the case in developing countries as well. For example, over 80 percent of Indian adults are now considered overfat, which means they have excess body fat negatively affecting their health. While this increases the risk of infections like Covid-19, the pandemic promoted even more junk food consumption, worsening the overfat prevalence worldwide. Beware of the myth *everything in moderation*. Does this include tobacco? Recent comments in research journals put this in perspective: *Sugar is the new tobacco*.

In addition to gut and immune problems, carbohydrate intolerance can lead to chronic inflammation, promoting pain, physical injury and disability, and chronic illness like Type 2 diabetes, hypertension, cancer, cardiovascular and Alzheimer's diseases, and many other health dysfunctions.

Junk food includes:

- Almost all bread, cereal, pasta, snacks, desserts, drinks and soda, and sports products.
- Packaged and prepared items commonly contain them (read the ingredients).
- Many products labeled natural, healthy, whole grain, low-fat and organic.
- Fast food and take-out items (even high-end restaurants require scrutiny).
- Meals on airlines, in schools and hospitals, and served at most social events.
- Sweetened alcoholic beverages.

It's important to realize that refined carbs often displace healthy vital nutrient-rich natural foods in the diet. These healthy foods include vegetables, raw nuts and seeds, proteins in whole eggs, meats, and cheese, and healthy fats. Our early ancestors ate mostly these natural foods for millions of years. This higher fat, moderate protein, and low carbohydrate dietary formula played a key role in developing the human brain.

For people who are carbohydrate-intolerant, even some natural foods can impair metabolism too, including corn, potatoes, fruit juice, dried fruit, grapes, pineapple, watermelon and bananas.

Many years ago, I developed a food challenge called the *Two-Week Test* to help people determine their carb sensitivity. This simple self-care guide is easily found online.

After eliminating all junk food, many report more mental and physical energy, better gut function, improved sleep, blood pressure, and sugar control, reduced depression and hormone imbalance, and lower weight and body fat. These benefits can start appearing within days.

Fats

Up to 70 percent of the brain is composed of fat. Eating healthy forms of fat while avoiding unhealthy ones promotes optimal brain function and performance. While U.S. and other government guidelines no longer have upper limits on natural fat consumption, a robust unhealthy market-driven fat-phobia still persists.

For decades, healthy dietary essential fats have been scientifically linked to better brain-body function, especially for learning, memory and aging, and to prevent chronic inflammation (a precursor to chronic disease, infection, disability and pain).

The best healthy fats include:

- Those that can reduce chronic inflammation in the same way (or better) that some drugs can. The most potent are EPA and DHA from cold-water natural fish (not farmed-raised). Fish and krill oils contain both essential fats, which are primary components of a healthy brain. Omega-3 vegetable oils such as flax don't contain EPA and DHA, although a healthy metabolism may convert small amounts to EPA. All omega-3s are very sensitive to destruction by heat and air.

- Extra-virgin olive and coconut oils are stable, along with butter, heavy cream, egg yolks and fats from grass-fed meats (corn-fed animals have high amounts of unhealthy fats).

Unhealthy fats include omega-6 oils like corn, safflower, soy, canola, and peanut, trans fats (hydrogenated), and those labeled mono- and diglycerides. They are commonly used in junk food and made even more unhealthy through oxidation when heated. These can displace stored healthy fats in the brain and body.

A single unhealthy ingredient can turn an otherwise healthy meal or snack into junk food.

Prescription and OTC Drugs

The proper use of medication is important in healthcare. Unfortunately, inappropriate and unsafe use is common, often with side effects in the brain, and usually replacing recommendations for healthy eating and lifestyle adjustments. Newer terms *polypharmacy* and *deprescribing* accompanied the dramatic rise in prescription and over-the-counter (OTC) drug use, including for children. Heavy marketing by drug companies targets both practitioners and consumers. About 70 percent of Americans regularly take at least one prescription drug, and more than half take two or more. Twenty-five percent or more exceed 20 daily meds! The use of OTC meds is even more common, far outpacing alcohol, heroin and cocaine combined. In many countries, prescription drugs are sold OTC.

In 2017, the World Health Organization launched an initiative to raise global awareness about inappropriate and hazardous prescribing. It aims to reduce the damage of avoidable meds, emphasizing that deprescribing can reduce drug-related harm, particularly in women who are more affected than men.

It's clearly possible to reduce drug doses, stop inappropriate drug therapies, and choose alternative safer approaches to improve health and increase the quality of life. While we should not be opposed to proper use of meds there should be greater focus on healthy living, especially through better eating habits.

Caffeine

As the world's most widely consumed and researched psychoactive substance, caffeine is a drug with substantial brain influence. Typically consumed in coffee and black tea, smaller amounts are in other teas and cacao, the raw material used to make chocolate. It's also available virtually everywhere, and junk food products like soft drinks are full of it too.

In many ways, caffeine is a potential wonder drug. It can improve many aspects of brain activity, especially creativity. Polymath physicist Henri Poincaré, in discovering his mathematical theory of Fuchsian groups, wrote that one evening contrary to custom he drank black coffee and could not sleep. Ideas "rose in crowds" and he felt them collide until pairs interlocked, resulting in a stable combination. By morning he woke to his theory as a complex equation.

For athletes, caffeine also can potentially enhance physical performance. One cup of coffee can increase oxygen consumption, blood circulation, muscle function, mitochondrial activity, conserve glycogen stores, and help recovery. For almost everyone, it can increase metabolic fat-burning for more energy and endurance while reducing excess body fat. It can affect genes that help convert stored white fat to brown, further amplify fat-burning, and increase healthy ketones for additional brain-body energy. Many of these benefits are reduced or eliminated with added sugar (natural or not). Despite claims, coffee won't dehydrate you.

Coffee can also slow the aging process and has been linked to lower incidences of many diseases.

Some people react poorly to caffeine, indicating it should be limited or avoided. It can overstimulate the brain, negatively affecting sleep, the gut, and potentially impair creativity. Some are sensitive even to decaf coffee or tea which still contains very small amounts of caffeine.

Alcohol

Many consider alcohol the most dangerous drug, even more so than heroin and cocaine. From the earliest human history, it's been more widely used than caffeine, tobacco, cannabis and other natural drugs. Alcohol easily influences brain function, impairing us with very small amounts. Still, many great artists made it part of their work including Beethoven, Poe and Socrates.

Research does show what many creatives infer, alcohol can improve creativity by helping reduce distractions. Many artists are over-aware of life's many sights, sounds, feelings and other sensory inputs competing for attention, which alcohol may moderate. But like other drugs, alcohol is not necessary for creativity. Hemingway was fond of alcohol, but reportedly refrained while writing.

While improving creativity, the same or lower amounts of alcohol can impair other areas of the brain, including executive function. Consider that even below legal limits, blood alcohol can impair driving. This apparent help-hurt alcohol paradox is associated with other health factors, too.

While smaller intakes of alcohol can reduce cardiovascular disease risk and mortality (premature death), abstinence can increase it. Moderate alcohol can increase cancer risks with small amounts lowering it. And, as alcohol can make us drowsy, it can impair sleep quality and quantity. As everyone knows, it should not be used before driving or operating other types of equipment.

For a long time, one drink for women and two for men was considered moderation (based on liver size and body weight). The new science of alcohol is lower: Light is the new moderate. While some people should never consume it, as we age our ability to break down alcohol in the stomach and liver is further reduced, increasing potential adverse risks. Alcohol is also metabolized most effectively up to about 6 p.m. and much less afterwards. One thing is certain — if a little is good a lot is not.

Despite their potential brain-body benefits, foods and drugs are often used differently:

- Cannabis and other psychedelics for recreation.
- Junk food is convenient, social and associated with love.
- Caffeine to counter low mental and physical energy.
- Alcohol for stress, distraction and to steer social settings.

Those choosing caffeine, cannabis or other psychedelics, or alcohol, should consider healthy use. Providing the body with nourishing food helps build a better brain at all ages. If prescription or OTC meds are recommended, talk with your health practitioner about potential alternatives, especially lifestyle modifications to obtain similar or better results.

Both ancient and modern wisdom directs us to key facts or core aspects of life: sex, drugs, music and food. Remember what the doorman said? Feed your head. Just choose wisely.

19

Heart Health and Music

As humans we certainly put our hearts into music. Ludwig van Beethoven is quite literally an example of this. Scientists have demonstrated that the distinctive rhythms in some of his compositions closely resemble those of heart rhythm disorders. This is particularly apparent in his "Les Adieux Sonata" and in the opening of his Fifth Symphony. Cardiologists consider these abnormalities as possible transcriptions of Beethoven's own heart arrhythmia, and that deafness may have enhanced his interoceptive awareness of the problem as composers often used their own heartbeats to guide tempo.

In addition to the sounds of an arrhythmia, numerous other heart problems have been associated with music. So much so that music is now being discussed as an underutilized tool in cardiology. Its wide-ranging use begins with instruction, where music's attributes and physiological effects make it an ideal way to learn about the important heart sounds. Students can more easily distinguish between the normal and abnormal through a stethoscope when heard as musical trills, grace notes and decrescendos associated with heart valves snapping closed and blood ebbing through leaky valves in cardiac plumbing disorders.

Music has also been useful in studying heart-brain health interactions, dispensing neurocardiac therapy, and applying the evidence of stress reduction whether from simple listening as prevention or while resting in bed after open-heart surgery.

Heart attacks, stroke and other cardiovascular diseases remain a leading cause of morbidity and death worldwide, across all genders and races in virtually every country, and these cardiac events are occurring at younger ages. Yet, up to 90 percent are preventable through relatively unused but simple lifestyle changes that reduce primary risk factors. Music can help in great part as it may be the only influence that reduces the most significant risk — the effects of physical, biochemical and mental-emotional stress through the brain's neurohormonal HPA axis.

Music not only has positive effects on the heart, but every cardiac cell, the blood vessels, the blood itself, and the circulatory connections that exchange air in our lungs by breathing. The health of the entire cardiovascular system can be powerfully influenced with a better musical brain, especially when combining movement and deep breathing as previously described using the Five-Minute Power Break and Meditative Dance.

The mother's heartbeat is perhaps the very first sensation we experienced in our earliest existence *in utero*. Following birth, this biofeedback beat allows babies, who appear to have jerky arm and leg motions, to be more rhythmic at the sound of music. This first natural aerobic heart rate training session encourages better neurological organized activity moving forward through adolescence and adulthood.

Our primal music-heart instinct is reflected in the heartbeat. Typically, the resting daytime pulse is around 60 beats per minute. Generally, stronger hearts are more efficient and beat slower, while others, including those less healthy, must work harder and are faster.

In fact, 60 appears to be a magic number. About 5,000 years ago, the Sumerians, who used song extensively, also developed timekeeping, mathematics and astronomy based on the same natural tempo of 60 as seconds per minute, and minutes per hour, through a *sexagesimal* system, a fraction based on sixtieths. Today, 60, and especially the related 120, remain as common intuitive tempos in performance and recorded music.

Heart rate continued throughout the ages to provide a natural unit of measure for musical time. In 1496, composer and music theorist Franchinus Gaffurius wrote that the proper measure of musical beat should be that of a healthy heart, and that the pulses of "fevered persons" are unequal in ways that worry physicians.

The modern mechanical metronome came into use around 1815, and, as one of the first notable composers to do so, Beethoven appeared to use it during the last 12 years of his life. When notating a *metronome mark*, this tempo appeared almost always after a piece was rehearsed and or performed several times. While initially writing a song, it seems Beethoven, like others, more than likely relied on the brain's instinctive tempo and his own heart.

Some musicians understand that metronome time is different from musical time.

In many instances, when interpreting musical emotion and other qualities, performers seldom play exactly on every beat. Instead, expressive, flexible *rubato* is sometimes used, a term referring to the rhythmic freedom to speed up and slow down to shape the tempo.

A well-functioning brain, especially the cerebellum as discussed earlier in relation to marching, can more easily maintain an accurate tempo to impart an appropriate emotion. While this is an important neuromuscular attribute, so is the ability to use rubato to flow with emotion. Stress can impair this process. Unfortunately, in today's rushed society, research shows many forms of music are performed up to 30 percent faster than 50 years ago, even if slower tempos are noted.

The widespread adoption of simple biofeedback devices can measure the cumulative stress on the cardiovascular system, such as an irregular rhythm, using *heart rate variability*, which reflects beat-to-beat intervals. Just as exercise and physical activity can be guided by heart rate monitoring to encourage adequate intensity while avoiding excess, these and other approaches can help guide the use of music in cardiac therapy, encouraging musical prescription, individualizing care and highlighting prevention.

Music can influence the heart in harmful ways, too. High volumes of any sound can impair cardiac health, inducing stress that constricts blood vessels and increases blood pressure proportionate to the crescendos. As noted earlier, excess loudness can promote deafness which is an additional risk factor for heart and other diseases.

The positive communal impact on human physiology also is potent: Individuals listening to the same songs tend to synchronize their circadian and heart rhythms, movements and breathing. This is exemplified by the work of Giuseppe Verdi, an Italian composer best known for his operas. Verdi's arias contained 10-second-long phrases known to emulate the body's natural blood pressure oscillations called *Mayer waves*. These and other brain responses also likely promote predictions and expectations during listening, especially storytelling, with fulfillment and violation of expectations contributing to the heartfelt meaning in music. As conscious and subconscious reactions, these are considered the progenitors of shared music-induced emotions, empathetic mirroring of external and internal experiences, and prompt pleasure via the brain's dopamine system.

The final moving movement of Beethoven's Symphony No. 9 is set to the text of Friedrich Schiller's poem "An die Freude" (Ode to Joy), imparting a powerful message of peace and unity to the world. On December 25, 1989,

Leonard Bernstein conducted this piece in the former East Berlin to celebrate the fall of the Berlin Wall, which divided East and West Germany during the Cold War, only a month earlier. The performance included musicians from Germany, Russia, the U.S., England, and France as a vibrant demonstration of peace and freedom during that moment in history. So, music fills our hearts in ways much more than the underutilized tool in cardiology; it's one that can also help bring us together as individuals to fix our world.

20

If Tomorrow Never Comes

Will we ever run out of music? While there are only 12 notes in the Western scale, we often play or sing these at higher and lower octaves. We can also sing and slur between notes, bend a guitar string, work the slide on a trombone, and make other unique musical sounds. Eastern scales include these notes, common in Indian and Arabic music. Regardless, the numbers seem limited, making unique music finite. But mathematics shows us that song possibilities still are in the googols: 10 to the 100th power, or 10 followed by 100 zeros.

Still, this leaves us to wonder what happens when the music's over? In a world of accumulating brain injuries, we could, as individuals and a species, lose our musical identity. T.S. Eliot wrote, "You are the music while the music lasts."

As individuals, when the music is unplugged, the many brain-body benefits can diminish or disappear. The downward spiral of dysfunction is already exemplified in populations of patients with personality disorders and other brain injuries, including amusia, and those living on junk music.

Bob Dylan said, "We're constantly being bombarded by insulting and humiliating music, which people are making for you the way they make those Wonder Bread products. Just as food can be bad for your system, music can be bad for your spiritual and emotional feelings. It might taste good or [be] clever, but in the long run, it's not going to do anything for you."

Like artificial food, artificial intelligence, or AI, is associated with unnatural music. AI music is literally music made by robots. It's a form of misinformation based on deception, and the inherent weaponization manipulates consumers and may invade copyright. For years AI has been infringing on brain function, including creativity and all the arts. Recently, scientists and tech industry leaders posted a warning on the Center for AI Safety's website: "Mitigating the risk of extinction from AI should be a global priority alongside other societal-scale risks such as pandemics and nuclear war." Add to this risk the loss of human music.

While we don't know the population-wide effects of losing real music, there are clues. For example, when songbirds lose their song, the outcome is devastating.

Can Your Bird Still Sing?

Like unborn humans, songbirds are affected by music even before hatching, coming into the world singing. This enables communication, cultural and social bonds, sexual selection, protection, and improved health and fitness. Music plays a key role in survival and the succession of a progressively stronger, more successful species. Knowing what to sing, however, is a learned experience influenced by previous generations, just as in humans.

When the music's over, not only are the songs lost but the species too.

The erosion of singing quality has led to severe declines in songbird populations as a preview to extinction. The loss of musicality includes reductions in song complexity and melodies, fewer syllables, and a lower number of both notes and frequency changes. One outcome is the loss of individuality with different birds singing very similar songs. This impairs sexual selection, the ability to find the best match.

The reasons songbird songs are impaired may be many, including deforestation and urban sprawl, noise pollution, poor food quality and other stress.

Over the past half century, human music has changed in ways not too dissimilar. Whether it's a natural pattern or red flag is unknown. However, parallel to these changes are others associated with a loss in health markers:

- Global rates of brain injury have risen significantly.
- Chronic illness is now the primary cause of death worldwide.
- Fertility rates have significantly dropped.
- Poor quality of life is on the increase.

- Life expectancy has recently taken a downturn.
- The Covid pandemic illustrated a resurgence in global instability.

You Say You Want a Revolution

When individuals rapidly combine the progress of past music with their own to create new sounds, while also influencing the future, researchers call it *revolutionary*. It reflects an expanding mind. We all have this potential to revolutionize our own personal creative selves in our journey through life.

In classical music, Igor Stravinsky's 1913 "The Rite of Spring" was such a revolutionary piece that it evoked riots following its first public performance. The Beatles revolutionized their own music while influencing dramatic changes across genres from classical to rap and everything in between. It began with the birth of rock n' roll in the 1950s beginning with the likes of Sister Rosetta Tharpe, Little Richard, Chuck Berry and Buddy Holly, then was amplified in the 60s by Dylan's switch to electric, and the British invasion of The Who, The Kinks, The Rolling Stones and others.

The tragic death of Buddy Holly in 1959 was referred to as "the day the music died" in Don McLean's 1971 hit song "American Pie." It reflected current deep cultural shifts and predicted critical musical changes. Did the revolution fail?

Active Versus Passive Music

A major difference between today's music and that from the 1950s into the 1970s is the transition from more active to more passive songs. Active music has a dynamic effect, leading us to think, act or believe in a proactive manner, and can help us build a better brain. Passive music, on the other hand, can have negative effects on the brain. Here are the main differentiations:

- Active music endows the brain with positive immediate and long-term benefits, and is a natural work of art. An active song enlists powerful personal memories and has obvious cultural influences. It makes us sit up and take note. We share in the memories of a love song, and in some way participate in a social issue.

- Passive music is conservative, junk music, more artificial, and influenced by the industry. A passive song is often promotional or background music, or a single component of the music is isolated and overstated, such as the driving beat only for dancing and exercise.

The recognition of active versus passive music is not new. Long ago Pete Seeger drove the effort to break down the passivity that often marks our encounter with music, encouraging its continual evolution. Most people know this intuitively. A healthy brain is drawn to active, feel-good music inspiring personal positive actions and influencing those around us.

This active versus passive relationship is an important brain-body response. Consider that those actively participating in any therapy respond better than those who don't. Or that passive TV watching versus active computer work significantly increases dementia risk. Listening to background music while talking or working, especially when we don't choose the music, often means we're unaware of what's playing. Gone are the days when people would gather for an active music listening session at home.

Producer Rick Rubin agrees that music's peak may have been the 1960s and 70s. This period corresponds to changes in drug use: from creative psychedelics to harmful habits. Rubin is the wise man of music, the go-to guy for singer-songwriters, and differentiates between the songs of yesterday and today. "Back then it was an artistic statement," he says. "Today a good song is one that gets on the radio; yesterday a good song was one people liked."

Many great songs in the 50s and 60s actively drove society but this phenomenon seemed to decline into passivity after the 1970s. Things are different today, says Robert Hilburn, a former *L.A. Times* music critic and *Rock and Roll Hall of Fame* nominating committee member, and author of books about John Lennon, Johnny Cash and Paul Simon. Bob's been on the scene since critiquing Elvis Presley's first album. He says that today, "It's what's catchy; music is much less an influence, less important on culture, playing less of a role."

Another factor is the singer-songwriter's influence, it's been decreasing every decade since the '70s. Most popular music today is controlled by the industry, with in-house songwriters mass-producing songs by committee — the source of most Billboard Hot 100 No. 1 hits. There have certainly been great singer-songwriters in the post-peak era, including Tom Petty, Tracy Chapman, Kurt Cobain, Prince, and millions of other lesser-knowns. But with more noise competing for our ears, it's reaching and influencing fewer brains.

Human Music Research

Some scientific studies support the ideas of a 60s-70s music peak. Songs between 1960 and 2010 were evaluated for personal taste and musical complexity, including variations in timbre, lyrics and chord changes. These began peaking in 1964 and concluded by around 1977. Post-70s music appeared more homogenized, containing less information with fewer variations. By 2000, timbre continued diminishing, as tempo, key and dynamic ranges weakened, and lyrics became less topical.

Another study that evaluated music between 1955 and 2010 showed a restriction of pitch sequences (less variety/simpler pitch progressions), homogenization of the timbral palette (with frequent timbres becoming more frequent) and growing average loudness levels (threatening a dynamic richness previously conserved). The conclusion was that later post-70s music ceased to have clear trends with little change. The researchers stated that one could take an old tune, simplify the chord progressions, add new modern instrument styles, and record it with increased loudness, and it could be easily perceived as new, fashionable and groundbreaking. It is astounding, for example, how many covers of Beatles songs have been recorded over the years; some people might think these songs are new, but they rarely live up to the original.

New research over a similar time frame shows changes that influence storytelling and melody — the instruments are literally drowning out the lyrics. An analysis of popular music's highest-ranked songs from the industry's Billboard Hot 100 chart shows lead vocals have become much quieter compared to the increasingly louder rhythmic beats. Vocals tell the story, conveying meaning, emotion and intellect, and also melody, a feature associated with memory. Along with louder instrumentation, vocal volumes hit a quiet low point around 1975 where they remain. Lowering lyrical volume and raising the rhythm, especially percussion and bass, can change the essence of a song, affecting both songwriter and listener. Lyrics have been a primary vehicle to convey emotion in music since the evolution of vocal language, which in great part replaced its gestural counterpart, especially with the advent of recorded music. This also can de-emphasize features of nonverbal musical language used for millions of years, such as tonality, facial expressions, postural movement and others noted earlier.

Industry Brain Injury

As songbirds are affected by stressful environments, the human brain is too, especially from the music industry. When artistic and commercial interests clash, it's not pretty. The industry often oversees such features as lyrics, song length, chord changes, and others in seeking control of the world's artistic expression and culture. Likewise for our listening behavior — but only when we don't control it ourselves. An important focus of this book has been to take charge of our brains by personalizing our music.

Music's global social-cultural language is vital for the health of everyone — and the planet. We don't want our brains censored by business or politics, nor do we want to be injured while missing out on expanding our minds with the freedom to think and express creatively.

The business of music streaming is controlled by those who manage the money, with few dollars actually going to artists. This commercialism is not new. Consider the industry's creation of The Monkees, Peter, Paul and Mary, and today's many planted media articles about their new albums or artists.

This dilution of creative expression was fought off by the Beatles, Joni Mitchell, Tom Petty, Neil Young, Billy Joel and others who voiced descent through their songs, maneuvering to success strictly due to artistry. Tom Waits battled with advertisers wanting to exploit the emotions his songs evoke. He sued Frito-Lay over using one of his songs to promote junk food, and was awarded $2.6 million.

While some great singer-songwriters may hit the music charts, most are non-industry underground independents, heard on streaming sites with less than minimal royalties. They typically write, record, publish and express themselves freely with fresh, heartfelt music. Touring was the primary source of revenue for these artists until Covid, and it has still not recovered.

Yet there is great hope. Many oldies have stood the test of time. New industry data shows that sales of these songs is about 70 percent of the U.S. music market, including The Beatles who remain among the most popular in all age groups.

There's an even more important point to emphasize. Despite similarities in human and songbird studies and their apple-orange comparisons, it's not where a music peak may or may not be, if there is one. It's whether:

- You like a song, album, artist or style.
- You listen to oldies that trigger memories.
- You're willing to venture into the unknown in search of surprising new music experiences.
- And that you don't stop.

The End

Many great musical masterpieces depict the end of life, among the most famous is the "Requiem in D minor" by Wolfgang Amadeus Mozart. Others are played after someone dies; Chopin's "Marche Funèbre" (Funeral March) was first performed at his own funeral. Most evoke feelings of sadness.

Among the famous last words in music is the Beatles' "The End," which concludes "and in the end the love you take is equal to the love you make." It's reportedly the last time all four Beatles recorded together, making it sad. Yet, it's a festive feel of joy and hope. Paul McCartney wrote the words, and years later said he liked the Irish traditional wake as a celebration because it included more laughing and joking.

For me, celebrating life in the moment with music is a daily routine. One of my lyrics is: "If tomorrow never comes we have today." First recorded in Nashville (and later as a world genre), when playing it live "If Tomorrow Never Comes" is a happy song with a bit of flamenco guitar crossed with a King Crimson feel.

We only have today — a chance to enhance the brain, experience memories and express ourselves. The answers are in the songs, making this moment of life real. Music is our moment.

It has been a privilege sharing stories from my musical journey with you, and I hope to see you along the way. Music really can turn your life into your own great song.

• • •

You can keep in touch through my website, MaffetoneMusic.com. In the B Sharp! book tab you'll find an extensive list of scientific references for easy searching, and more. On the home page there's a link to my YouTube video channel. And all my music is free to members.

Printed in Great Britain
by Amazon